Maritime Archaeology for Beginners

Maritime Archaeology for Beginners

Sila Tripati

KAVERI

Kaveri Books
4697/5-21A, Ansari Road
New Delhi - 110002 (India)
Tel.: 011-2328 8140, 2324 5799
e-mail: kaveribooks@vsnl.com

First published in English by Kaveri Books, 2009

ISBN 13: 978-81-7479-103-0

Layout & Typeset in *Balaram* by *Sparsh Communications, Delhi*
Printed at *Salasar Imaging Systems, Delhi.*

PRINTED IN INDIA

Dedicated to the pioneers who nurtured this discipline

Foreword

Sila Tripati (2009) Maritime Archaeology for Beginners.

Around the world, in every country and among people of every origin, gender and age, more people than ever are interested in the fascinating discoveries being made by maritime archaeologists, discoveries which daily shed new light upon the links between communities enabled by the sea. However, there are also many different threats to our shared global maritime cultural heritage, and these too are growing. Maritime Archaeology for Beginners is thus to be warmly welcomed and its author thanked for his hard work in producing this volume, for the need for accessible works explaining the principles and practice of maritime archaeology is greater now than ever before. It is for these reasons that I was delighted, and deeply honoured, to be invited to write this foreword.

In this one slim volume, anyone interested in the exciting world of maritime archaeology will find answers to all those questions they have ever wanted to know but were perhaps afraid to ask. Meanwhile, those already familiar with the field will find here a useful 'ready reference' of sources and concepts, tools and techniques, names and places. The fact that this book is written by a practicing maritime archaeologist makes the work all the more timely and useful; here are the answers from those who really know, compiled from hard-won knowledge. This work is also of use to far more than simply those based within India; major portions of this book will be of interest and use to students of maritime archaeology across the world, reinforcing once again how communities so often seemingly distant and different are interlinked through the presence of the sea.

As Sila Tripati demonstrates, while maritime archaeology may be a relatively young discipline in India, it is as rich and vibrant as its 'older sibling' of terrestrial archaeology. Indian maritime archaeology has, and continues to make, a consistent and significant contribution to our understanding of the history of the world. Scholars are now exploring every time period and location, from the earliest human origins in prehistory, through voyages of exploration and trade, right up to the present day, recording surviving boatbuilding traditions and fishing communities.

The Institute of Archaeology in London has a long and distinguished history of contact with India, begun through the pioneering work of our founding director, Sir Mortimer Wheeler, who did so much to foster professionalism and cooperation in and between our two great countries. The Institute also has a long history of involvement in maritime archaeology, through the work of that other, less well-known pioneer Joan du Plat Taylor, our librarian during the 1960s and 1970s. Under her inspiration, a generation of young researchers was encouraged to enter and advance the newly emerging discipline of maritime archaeology, and the Institute became known as the 'Pharos of Bloomsbury', a beacon of good practice named after the neighbourhood of London where the Institute is based. Stepping forward thirty years, we are now lucky to have such beacons of research spread across the globe, where a new generation of maritime archaeologists such as myself have joined established researchers in their endeavours. One such 'pharos' is undoubtedly the Maritime Archaeology Centre, National Institute of Oceanography in Goa. Here, dedicated scholars such as Sila Tripati with many of his colleagues, advance the science and art of maritime archaeology, now and, with luck, long into the future.

I warmly recommend this book to all who come across it, and wish everyone good luck in their own explorations of the maritime world which we inhabit. The study of maritime archaeology is as endless as it is fascinating, and all who come into contact with the discipline are enriched by its tales of human endeavour and progression.

Joe Flatman
Institute of Archaeology
University College London
UK

Acknowledgements

This book could not have been written without using the published material and ideas of many scholars, discussions with colleagues and associates of India and abroad including my own colleagues at NIO, Goa. I am also indebted to all my teachers, associates, scientists and friends who showed me the way to approach archaeological problems. Dr Satish R. Shetye, Director, National Institute of Oceanography and Shri K. H. Vora, Scientist-in-Charge, Marine Archaeology Centre has extended all the facilities and constant encouragement which made publication of this work a possibility.

Many scholars have provided sincere and involved help for quite some time. It is with my pleasure and gratitude that I name a few of them: Professor George Bass, Valerie Fenwick, Paula Martin, Joe Flatman, Cheryl Ward, Sarah Arenson, Thijs J. Maarleveld, Harry Tzalas, Masaaki Kimura, Hanae Sasaki, Bruno Werz, Johan Rönnby, Marcus Hjulhammar and Wendy van Duivenvoorde. It is indeed my privilege to say thanks to Dr C. Margabandhu, Professor Shereen Ratnagar, Dr M. Dileep Kumar, Franco Fernando, Dr Sridhar Iyer and Mrs Ramola Antao for their valuable suggestions on the manuscript. I have taken help from many people who have contributed in one way or other to the book, I am obliged to them. I am also thankful to my colleagues namely Dr A. S. Gaur, Sundaresh, S. N. Bandodker of Marine Archaeology Centre for their support at every stage of this work. The book contains many figures, photographs, half tones, etc. Shri Dusmant Maharana, S. N. Bandodker, S. B. Chitari, Arun Mahale, Ravindra Uchil, Shamkant Akerkar, Kamlakar Chitari, Uday Javali, Pramod Pawaskar, Sheikh Ali Karim and Mahesh Mochemadkar have shown tremendous patience and have provided me with wonderful prints. This is NIO's Contribution No: 4464

Contents

Preface

Until recently, there have been few scholarly monographs and research articles by scholars and researchers involved in maritime archaeological studies in India. Furthermore, not many attempts have been made to pass on this acquired knowledge to graduate and postgraduate students of Archaeology, History, Anthropology and related disciplines, or to amateur divers, scholars and others seeking acquaintance with this nascent discipline. For all such readers, I hope this book, 'Maritime Archaeology for Beginners' will serve as a useful introduction and incentive to further study. Hence the major part of this book answers questions starting with 'what', 'when', 'who', 'how' and 'why'.

Both maritime and underwater archaeology are relatively new sciences that are swiftly developing because new technological advances are available that allow oceanographers and archaeologists to explore deeper depths of ocean which were previously unreachable.

The author has endeavoured to include every major aspect of maritime archaeology. In compiling this book about 200 questions and answers have been incorporated which are felt to be essential for students and researchers. Of course, not every question on underwater or maritime archaeological aspects has been answered. However, a comprehensive report of all sites of India where maritime archaeological explorations have been carried out by the Marine Archaeology Centre of the NIO, India has been included.

In contrast with other sciences maritime archaeology has developed recently and was recognised only in the later nineteenth century. Maritime and underwater archaeology is an emerging discipline; hence some explanation of these terms 'maritime' and 'underwater' archaeology is required for better understanding by readers. Underwater archaeology is the study of archaeology which includes the submerged environments such as sunken ships, ports and habitational sites and cities which existed on land years ago but are now underwater. The foremost objective of underwater archaeology is to explore and excavate such sites and correlate the finds with various historical events of mankind, whereas maritime archaeology is concerned with every aspect of the maritime activities of human beings in rivers, lakes, seas and oceans. On the other hand, archaeologists who are involved in this field do not always adhere to these definitions; some refer to their work as 'marine', 'nautical', 'shipwreck' or 'boat' archaeology.

In some countries highly sophisticated tools and equipment are used for both shallow and deepwater explorations, but questions related to those are not listed. Only questions which relate to Indian waters and others which are felt important for the readers are incorporated.

My purpose will be fulfilled if this book motivates readers to go on to others that provide more insights and information.

Sila Tripati
January 2009

Abbreviations

AIMA	Australian Institute of Maritime Archaeology
ASI	Archaeological Survey of India
AUV	Autonomous Underwater Vehicles
BAIMA	Bulletin of the Australasian Institute for Maritime Archaeology
BCD	Buoyancy Compensator Device
CNA	Council for Nautical Archaeology
CNANS	National Center for Nautical and Underwater Archaeology
DGPS	Differential Global Positioning System
DPV	Diver Propulsion Vehicle
DOD	Department of Ocean Development
DST	Department of Science and Technology
EIA	Environmental Impact Assessment
GPS	Global Positioning System
HOV	Human-Occupied vehicles
IJNA	International Journal of Nautical Archaeology
INA	Institute of Nautical Archaeology
IPA	Portuguese Institute of Archaeology
ISBSA	International Symposium on Boat and Ship Archaeology
MAC	Marine Archaeology Centre
NARA	National Aquatic Resources Agency
NAS	Nautical Archaeology Society
NAUI	National Association of Underwater Instructors
NIO	National Institute of Oceanography
NIOT	National Institute of Ocean and Technology
NISA	Netherlands Institute for Ship and Underwater Archaeology
PADI	Professional Association of Diving Instructors
ROV	Remotely Operated Vehicle
SAIMA	Southern African Institute of Maritime Archaeology
SCA	Supreme Council of Antiquities
SCUBA	Self Contained Underwater Breathing Apparatus
SDDE	Surface Demand Diving Equipment
SMA	Society for Marine Archaeology
SNR	Society for Nautical Research
UGC	University Grants Commission
VOC	Dutch East India Company
WAMM	Western Australia Maritime Museum

CHAPTER ONE

GENERAL AWARENESS AND DEVELOPMENTS OF MARITIME ARCHAEOLOGY

1. What is maritime archaeology?

Maritime archaeology is the scientific study of past seafaring from the material remains of man and his activities on the sea. It is an interdisciplinary study, which acts as a bridge between humans and the sciences. Maritime archaeology is a discipline that studies human interaction with seas, lakes and rivers through the study of ships and boats, port installations, cargoes, material remains and submerged landscapes. It is a distinct and emerging field within the broader discipline of archaeology. Maritime archaeological investigations are also carried out in seas, rivers and lakes and its discoveries are sometimes associated with historical events.

2. What are the other names of maritime archaeology?

Maritime archaeology is also known as 'underwater', 'marine' and 'nautical' archaeology. There is often a confusion over the use of the terms 'maritime', 'underwater', 'marine' and 'nautical'. All are valid terms for different aspects. One aspect of underwater archaeology is the study of the past through any submerged remains such as shipwrecks, habitations or ports. In the recent past, the new nomenclature 'Hydro-archaeology' has been coined to include all aspects of maritime archaeology where water plays a great role.

3. What are the differences between underwater, marine and nautical archaeology?

'Nautical archaeology' is a study of different types of seagoing vessels, their construction techniques, maritime technology, varieties of practices and usages; whereas 'maritime archaeology' encompasses all kinds of maritime activities, which include trade, commerce, water transport technology, seafaring, coastal settlements, ports and harbours, aspects related to maritime cultures including socio-economic, religious and political elements of past societies. Maritime archaeology, while similar to 'underwater archaeology', goes beyond because it includes all disciplines related to this aspect covering maritime and nautical archaeology, not necessarily under water. It is equally concerned with archaeological remains found on the coastal, intertidal zone and on the seabed. 'Marine archaeology' exclusively deals with archaeology in the sea.

4. What is riverine archaeology?

Unlike seas and oceans from the earliest times, the river played a significant role in the line of communication. Riverine archaeology specialises in the study of artefacts of early river traffic and archaeological evidence observed along river banks and traces of abandoned log boats, rafts and barges used at one time for carrying cargo and passengers. Furthermore, port installations, anchors, slipways, wharfs and docks are found along the riverbanks. The archaeological study related to river traffic in terms of trade and communication and associated findings is known as riverine archaeology.

5. What is deep sea archaeology?

Deep sea archaeology is beyond the reach of divers, so the amount of archaeology which can be achieved is severely limited. It is a recent development in maritime archaeological studies and started in 1988 with the discovery of ancient deep water trade routes between the Roman seaport of Ostia and ancient Carthage. The exploration between 1988 and 1997 brought to light the largest number of ancient shipwrecks ever found in the deep sea. In an area of 210 km^2 in all eight shipwrecks were located in 1000 m water depth datable from 100 BC to AD 400. The discovery was possible because of available sophisticated deepwater equipments and techniques namely, ROVs, AUVs and submersibles. More recently, two more shipwrecks of the Phoenician period, probably 2700 years old, have been located in 450 m water depth about 55 km north of Egypt.

6. What is submerged site archaeology?

It is maritime archaeological study specialising in the study of submerged sites both in lakes and seas. The sites which once stood above water and are now submerged either due to subsidence of land, rising water levels or a combination of both. Submerged sites exist in shallow waters and are common in some areas and rare in others, depending on the geological history. Many submerged prehistoric, historical habitational and ports sites have been explored and excavated all along the coastline of the world. This happens only with low lying cities and ports and several instances have come to light from the Mediterranean Sea that occurred due to subsidence. In Jamaica one such incident occurred due to the earthquake in AD 1692 in which 90 percent of the town of Port Royal sank into the sea. Similarly, some habitational sites in Switzerland located on low ground at the side of lakes have been submerged. They date from the Neolithic period to the Early Iron Age.

7. What are the differences between land and maritime archaeology?

Basically there are no differences between land and maritime archaeology. The objectives of both disciplines are the same: 'Let us uncover the glory of the unknown past of human activities buried under the surface both in land and underwater'. However, the differences between land and maritime archaeology are the environment in which the work is carried out, the working principles and procedures, methods and equipment. Maritime archaeology is a part and parcel of archaeology because archaeology itself is a broad discipline. Land archaeological excavations were started in India in 1865 by the Archaeological Survey of India, (ASI) whereas maritime archaeological studies commenced in 1981 by NIO, Goa. Since then maritime archaeological explorations and excavations have been carried out at these sites (Fig. 1).

Fig. 1 Map showing the location of sites mentioned in the text

8. What are the differences between land and underwater archaeological sites?

An archaeological site is defined as the concentration of material remains of human activities. Land archaeological sites can be located easily because a number of artefacts such as pottery, structures, coins, seals, sealing, sculptures, tools, objects from other countries, inscriptions, etc., are visible, often in vegetation. Potsherds and other artefacts may be scattered all over a site. Moreover, a number of artefacts can be seen exposed soon after the monsoons at rain gullies. Archaeological evidence varies from site to site depending upon the period and nature of the site.

A wide range of underwater archaeological sites have been located and explored all over the world. Each underwater site will have a different environment and finds may belong to different periods. Hence while studying individual site(s) much attention should be paid to the context and the period. For instance, a shipwreck exploration may reveal the remains of a ship, which includes timber, cargo, belongings of crew, pottery and anchors. Studies of these finds can provide information on its ports of call, origin of objects on board, provenance of the ship and other details including where the ship was built. Similarly, exploration of a port site can yield remains of anchors, pottery, coins, structural remains, etc. Further research on these finds would provide evidence for the maritime contacts of the port, export and import, contact between traders and mariners, types of vessels which called on the port and causes of its decline.

9. What is the importance of underwater archaeological sites?

Underwater archaeological sites are as important as land archaeological sites to reconstruct the maritime history of the country and contacts with other countries. Sometimes remains of port installations and habitational sites can be seen on the shore or intertidal zone because once upon a time those were on land; subsequently some unprecedented natural phenomena such as submergence of land, rise of sea level, coastal erosion, accretion or reclamation of land for industrial activities might has submerged them. Material evidence lasts for a longer duration under water without any disintegration, than on land sites. Table-1 shows a comparison between material disintegration on land and underwater. This material evidence indicates directly and indirectly the importance of underwater archaeological sites.

Often, artefacts or objects are preserved under water without having been disturbed as artefacts on land often are. On account of this, underwater

Table-1 (Survival of archaeological evidence on land as well as underwater)

Nature of Evidence	Organic/ Inorganic
1. Iron	Inorganic
2. Textile	Organic
3. Basketry	Organic
4. Skin	Organic
5. Plants	Organic
6. Carbonised	Organic
7. Invertibrates	Organic
8. Copper Aloy	Inorganic
9. Wood	Organic
10. Shell	Organic
11. Glass	Inorganic
12. Antler	Organic
13. Bone	Organic
14. Stone	Inorganic
15. Pottery	Inorganic
16. Flint	Inorganic

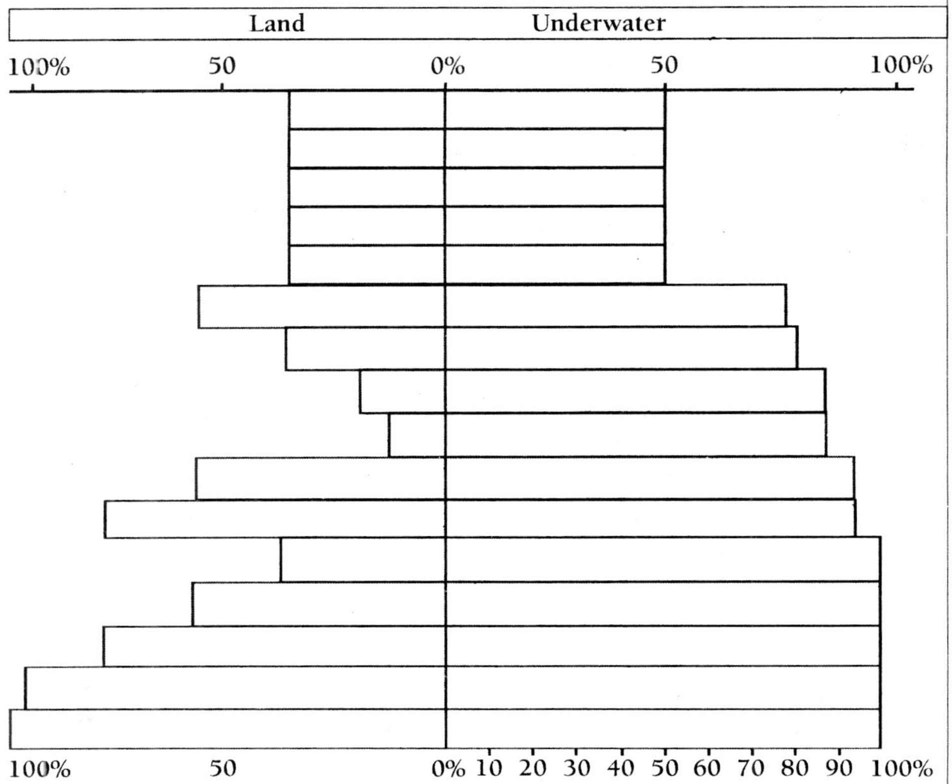

archaeological sites are also known as 'time capsules', with their artefacts being from approximately the date. At times clues available on land sites do not necessarily give accurate information about what exactly happened at any specific period; instead they indicate the changes and processes over time. Under these circumstances it becomes difficult to understand the nature of a site at any particular stage. The answer to the oft-repeated question, 'why make archaeology even more difficult by trying to do it underwater' could be that the water hides, preserves, protects and traps clues of archaeology, which are often not found on land sites. Using our ingenuity to find these clues and evidence seems a small price to pay.

10. Is treasure hunting a part of maritime archaeology?

Treasure hunting or salvaging of cargo from lost ships goes back much farther than marine archaeological research. Treasure hunting is absolutely not a part of maritime archaeology. It is the commercial search for, and exploitation of, economically valuable items from historic wrecks. The people involved in this activity are wrongly directed into an illegal practice. This practice is threatening our underwater cultural heritage because it destroys evidence for ever. If such treasure is salvaged with no archaeological documentation, in the worst case looted, unique information is lost for ever. Neither governments nor any authorities encourage treasure hunting. Treasure hunting or treasure salvage is not a scientific approach, hence it should not be confused with maritime archaeology; such activities should be curbed and stopped. Attempts should be made to make everyone understand the importance of our heritage.

11. What are the jobs of maritime archaeologists?

The primary job of maritime archaeologists is to undertake exploration, excavation, documentation, preservation, interpretation and reconstruction of the maritime history of mankind and preserve it for posterity. Maritime archaeologists undertake exploration to bring to light the unknown maritime history of the country, to reveal the maritime connections with other overseas countries, and to collect information on shipwrecks. Over the years maritime archaeologists have made tremendous progress both in tools and technologies for undertaking underwater explorations. Similar developments have been made to document underwater discoveries both in shallow as well in deeper waters. The availability of new tools make it easy for maritime archaeologists to achieve the desired goals.

12. How can one become a maritime archaeologist?

The candidate should have a Masters Degree in Archaeology or Ancient Indian History, Culture and Archaeology or History or Anthropology from a recognised university. In case of India, the desirable qualification would be a PG Diploma in Archaeology from the Institute of Archaeology, Archaeological Survey of India (ASI), New Delhi. The candidate should have knowledge of diving or should undergo a course on diving, which is a MUST (highly essential) for undertaking underwater exploration for maritime archaeological studies. Whereas some foreign universities offer degrees and diplomas in maritime archaeology, no such facility is available in India. Besides archaeology there are many auxiliary branches like marine geology, chemistry, diving and seamanship, nautical engineering and shipbuilding technology, draughtsman, electronics, marine survey, preservation, conservation and which facilitate maritime archaeological studies directly or indirectly. For instance, chemistry helps in conservation and preservation of artefacts, and shipbuilding knowledge helps in identifying parts of the vessel, its construction and its reconstruction. Marine Geology supports maritime archaeology in studying sea level rise, coastal erosion, accretion, etc.

13. What subjects are taught within maritime archaeology?

The subjects taught differ very much from university to university and institute to institute. A browse of the websites of the University of Southern Denmark, the Norwegian Technical University, University College London, the University of St Andrews, the University of Bristol, the University of Bournemouth, and Flinders University, South Australia shows variety of subjects taught within maritime archaeology. For instance, the Masters Degree syllabus in Maritime Archaeology of Southampton University consists of: scope, source materials, theory and methodology; Marine geoarchaeology; Strategies and techniques of underwater and intertidal excavation and recording; Ethnography of maritime communities; Technology and tradition of watercraft; Maritime trade and exchange; and Conservation of maritime heritage. In contrast, Flinders University teaches the archaeology of maritime trade and industry and includes both land based and underwater sites, such as jetties, ports and shipwrecks and the study of ships, shipping and the construction and operation of all types of prehistoric and historic watercraft.

14. Does maritime archaeology involve fieldwork and training in diving?

Generally, no university offers training in diving directly, but some universities liaise with diving organisations to offer training to students. Similarly, for fieldwork Flinders University has a field school, but most universities simply ensure that students have an opportunity to join someone else's field school. The students of INA get the opportunity to participate both in fieldwork as well as diving. There are some institutes and universities involved in shipwreck excavation allow students of different countries to participate in underwater exploration. For instance, archaeology students of Portugal and students of other countries participate in the CNANS fieldwork and diving. Diving regulations are so tight in the UK that it is difficult for students to get experience unless they already have professional diving qualifications.

15. Name some organisations where such courses are offered in India and elsewhere?

In the past NIO, Goa organised training courses on maritime archaeology with a series of lectures on related aspects including fieldwork and diver training. Currently the Indian Navy offers diving courses as do private diving companies in India, issuing PADI certificates. However, none of them include theory and fieldwork.

The training programme created by the Nautical Archaeology Society enables the public to learn more about archaeology and offers an opportunity to practice the techniques required on land and under water. Along with other non-governmental organisations involved in maritime archaeological research, NAS aims to preserve the underwater heritage by involving people from diverse disciplines such as amateur divers, biologists, geologists, historians and others having an interest in it. Further, NAS has links with AIMA in Australia, CNANS in Portugal and many other organisations round the world. NAS recognised scholars conduct the theory classes on site and teach archaeological diving to students.

16. What are the career prospects of a maritime archaeologist?

There are potential career prospects in maritime archaeology, in the sense that very few shipwrecks have been excavated in the world and the rest are yet to be explored and excavated. There may be many reasons for wrecks not to be explored and excavated. One reason is lack of funds, but useful jobs are to be found within archaeological units and museums, both private and government.

Working in these fields may not be totally maritime, but maritime skills are occasionally needed. For instance, India has a 5,716 km long coastline but only between five and seven archaeologists from two government organisations are involved in maritime archaeological research. Many maritime archaeologists are academics who teach in university departments of history, anthropology, classics and other related fields. Similarly, there are some countries where no institutes or organisations deal with maritime archaeology but scholars and researchers from other countries undertake maritime archaeological research in the form of projects and assist the respective governments to set up maritime archaeological research units.

17. What are the popular web sites on maritime archaeology?

There are several web sites on maritime archaeology and allied disciplines. The following web sites can be recommended for information: http://www.nasportsmouth.org.uk of the Nautical Archaeology Society (NAS), UK; http://www.inadiscover.com of the Institute of Nautical Archaeology (INA), USA and Bodrum, Turkey; http://www.nautarch.tamu.edu of the Texas A&M University, USA; http://www.aima.iinet.net.au of the Australasian Institute for Maritime Archaeology (AIMA), Fremantle, Australia; http://www.flinders.edu.au of Flinders University of Australia; http://www.nio.org of the National Institute of Oceanography, India; and http://www.subarch.com of Nordic Underwater Archaeology. Several links to other maritime archaeology sites are offered via these web sites. Links to other sites can also be accessed by typing the name of the organization or institute in any web search engines. A number links on maritime archaeology can be accessed from www.Google.com.

18. What periodicals on maritime archaeology are published?

Several books and encyclopaedias have been published on maritime archaeology. Apart from books, the periodicals are: *The International Journal of Nautical Archaeology* (IJNA) published by the Nautical Archaeology Society, UK, http://www.blackwell-synergy.com/loi/ijna; the *Bulletin of the Australasian Institute for Maritime Archaeology* (BAIMA) and *quarterly newsletters*; *Mariner's Mirror*, published by the Society for Nautical Research (SNR), UK; the *Journal of Maritime Archaeology*, published by http://www.springerlink.com/content/1557-2285; *Rivista di Studi Liguri* was published by the Maritime Archaeology Research Centre of Italy prior to1980; the *Newsletter* of AIMA; *The INA Quarterly* and *The INA Annual* of INA, USA; and the *Newsletter of NAS*.

World Archaeology, http://www.informaworld.com/smpp/title~content has published many issues on titles related to maritime archaeology. Frequently articles on maritime archaeology are published in: *Antiquity*, http://antiquity.ac.uk; the *American Journal of Archaeology*, www.ajaonline.org; and *Man and Environment* http://prehistoryindia.com. In India, the Society for Marine Archaeology of NIO formerly published the *Journal of Marine Archaeology,* but this has been temporarily stopped, whereas the *Journal of Indian Ocean Archaeology*, New Delhi, has published the archaeology of the Indian Ocean countries since 2004.

Some organisations publish the proceedings of their conferences; examples are: *Tropis*, the proceedings of the Hellenic Institute for the Preservation of Nautical Tradition, Greece and the *Proceedings of the International Symposium on Boat and Ship Archaeology* (ISBSA) hosted every three years by a different country.

19. When, where and who started maritime archaeology?

Maritime archaeology as a discipline started in the 19th century but academically it was taken under water after 1950. Maritime archaeology was born in the Mediterranean Sea. In terms of being recognised as an academic discipline, the founder of underwater archaeology is generally agreed to be Professor George Bass, who as a young graduate student at the University of Pennsylvania pioneered the discipline more than 40 years ago. He was invited to take over direction of a Bronze Age shipwreck in the eastern Mediterranean Sea off the Turkish coast. His shipwreck excavations off Turkey became models for other archaeologists.

20. In what way did Peter Throckmorton contribute to the beginning of maritime archaeology?

Peter Throckmorton was the first scholar to take archaeology to the seabed. The discovery of various types of metal, terracotta and other artefacts on ancient wreck sites made him realise the need for these underwater historic sites to be excavated and interpreted by archaeologists. Subsequently he learned to dive and in 1958 heard of the discovery of a bronze bust of Demeter by a fisherman. The bronze bust of Demeter had been found in the sea off Bodrum, Turkey. Other fishermen informed him of their discovery of copper ingots off Cape Gelidonya, leading him to conclude that it might date to the prehistoric period. It was this discovery which prompted the determination of Peter Throckmorton together with Joan du Plat Taylor to create an academic discipline based on shipwreck archaeology. Joan prompted Peter to find a young archaeologist who could dive and take over the archaeological direction of the Cape Gelidonya shipwreck. At the end of 1959 Peter managed to interest George Bass in the wreck. He raised funds from various sources and exploration of the wreck site started. Under George's direction a team was formed in which Joan du Plat Taylor and Honor Frost took part, while Peter contributed the published report. The Cape Gelidonya shipwreck became a pivotal scientific study. Peter continued to explore the seabed and published a number of underwater sites ranging from the Roman period to the 18th century AD. Among his publications the most popular were: *The Lost Ships* (1965), *Shipwrecks and Archaeology: the Unharvested Sea* (1969), while *History from the Sea* (1987) was edited by him.

21. How was maritime archaeology started?

Maritime archaeology is not really a case of sudden invention, but a gradual development in standards of excavation. The invention of scuba diving enabled it to be practised under water.

Prior to scuba diving, helmeted salvors salvaging modern shipwrecks and sponge divers collecting sponges occasionally came across ancient artefacts. This attracted interest among archaeologists and amateur divers. However the scenario changed with the advent of scuba equipment and the growth of sport diving. Two separate developments took place in the 1950s which changed the future of maritime archaeology: the archaeologist took more interest in diving and learned to dive; simultaneously a large number of divers who were interested in doing archaeology under water became archaeologists.

In his book '*Archaeology Under Water*' (1966), George Bass has described the history of underwater archaeology. In his recent edited book '*Beneath the Seven Seas*' (2005), he has further described how this discipline started in other parts of the world. The pioneers of diving, Jacques Yves Cousteau followed by both French and Italian divers, made early attempts at the excavation of Roman shipwrecks off the coasts of France and Italy and developed some good techniques, but no excavation was carried to completion and in no case was the work directed by a diving archaeologist. Around 1960, a number of developments occurred. In 1960 George Bass went to Cape Gelidonya, Turkey to excavate the Bronze Age shipwreck datable to 1200 BC. Five Viking ships were recovered from Roskilde Fjord, Denmark in

1965. The warship *Vasa* (*Wasa*) was raised from the worm free waters of the Baltic Sea in Stockholm Harbour, Sweden in 1961. The recovery and preservation of the *Mary Rose* was another landmark in maritime archaeology. *Mary Rose* was the large warship of King Henry VIII, lost in 1545 and raised in 1982.

22. Which was the first shipwreck explored by maritime archaeologists and what are its findings?

The Cape Gelidonya wreck on the Southern coast of Turkey was the first shipwreck excavated by maritime archaeologists. The wreck dated to 1200 BC was that of a merchant vessel. The remains lay at a depth of 26-28 m. Excavations yielded a ton of copper ingots from Cyprus, remnants of tin ingots, broken bronze agricultural tools from Cyprus and bronze swage, stone hammerheads, many stone polishers and a whetstone. The wreck also revealed Mycenaean, Cypriot and Syrian pottery; Syrian stone mortars; and a Syrian merchant's cylinder seal. The nationality of the crew was from the Near East (Canaanite?) which was indicated by a ship's terracotta oil lamp, stone mortars, seals and an anchor. Finds from the shipwreck are displayed in the Underwater Archaeology Museum, Bodrum, Turkey.

23. Who were the team members of the Cape Gelidonya shipwreck excavation?

The wreck was located in 1954 by Kemal Aras a sponge diver from Bodrum, Turkey. After getting information from Kemal, Peter Throckmorton relocated the site in 1959 and requested the University of Pennsylvania Museum, USA, to undertake its excavation as the first true and complete underwater archaeological excavation of an ancient shipwreck, it was also the first directed by a diver archaeologist and the first excavation conducted following the standards of terrestrial excavation. The international team comprised: Director George F. Bass; Assistant Director (diving) Peter Throckmorton; Assistant Director (non-diving) Joan du Plat Taylor; chief diver Frederic Dumas; photographers Peter Throckmorton and Herb Greer; cataloguer Ann Bass; divers Claude Duthuit, Waldemar Illing and Yuksel Egdemir.

24. How was maritime archaeology started in Australia?

The discovery of two 17th century shipwrecks in 1963 laid the foundation of maritime archaeology in Australia. At the same time the significance of shipwreck archaeology was included in the Museum Act and later amended to the Maritime

Archaeology Act of 1973 to protect shipwrecks prior to 1900. The Western Australian Maritime Museum (WAMM) was given the responsibility for administering the act. Maritime archaeological explorations were started in 1970 with the survey of the East India Company ship *Trial* (1622), the oldest known shipwreck in Australia. Subsequently, *Vergulde Draeck* (1656) and *Batavia* (1629) were excavated. The Western Australian State Maritime Archaeology Act 1973 is still in operation and deals with maritime archaeological sites including remains of ships, relics or structures both in water and on land. With the combined efforts of state agencies and state maritime archaeological associations, the Australian Institute of Maritime Archaeology (AIMA) developed in 1970. In the year 1981 the universities of Australia and WAMM initiated graduate diplomas in maritime archaeology, including courses in maritime archaeology, conservation, material science, oceanography, marine survey. Afterwards, the AIMA started publishing annual bulletins, quarterly newsletters and occasionally special publications on marine archaeology.

25. How did maritime archaeology start in China and Southeast Asia?

From the perspective of maritime archaeology these geographical regions have suffered much from treasure hunters. Among other wrecks, artefacts were salvaged from the *Geldermalsen* (1747) in Indonesian waters and sold for a high price. The Philippines National Museum undertakes maritime archaeological research in the Philippines. The government grants permission to treasure hunters to undertake surveys. Over a period of time, the *San Diego* (1600) and the *Griffin* (1761) shipwrecks have been excavated by the National Museum in collaboration with World Wide First, a non-commercial organisation. Besides these shipwrecks, the National Museum has discovered and explored nine Butuan boats. The Butuan boats are of lashed-lug construction similar to archaeological finds in Malaysia and Sumatra. With regard to the maritime archaeology of China, the majority of publications are in Chinese and only a few are in English. The *Quanzhou* ship has been excavated and documented. The Fa Sui site was excavated and a buried ship of the Song Dynasty was found at Ningbo. In Thailand the first shipwreck survey was started in 1975 by a joint Thai-Danish team off Ko Khram. Exploration brought to light more than 5,000 potsherds which mostly consist of Thai, Sukhothai, Sawankhalok and Vietnamese wares. The site was explored again in 1987 in order to collect timber and ceramic samples and the site was found to be intact, with no evidence of looting. The *Ko Kradat* wreck was explored in Trat province and yielded porcelain belonging to the Ming dynasty (AD 1522-1566) and Wanli period (AD 1573-1619). Shipwrecks, namely the Ko

Si Chang 1, 2 and 3, have been explored in Chonburi Province and remains have been documented. The Pattaya wreck site was explored in 1982. The hull was uncovered and the bow half of the site was excavated. The *Rang Kwien* shipwreck was ransacked by looters, but investigation by the Fine Arts Department between 1978 and 1981 yielded copper coins, copper ingots, elephant tusks, bells and ceramics.

26. How did maritime archaeology start in Egypt?

Underwater exploration in Egypt was begun in the 1960s by an officer of the Egyptian Navy looking for remains of the Pharos of Alexandria. It was continued by the Franco-Egyptian expedition under Jean Yves Empereur in the 1980s with the search for Napoleon's fleet of sunken ships at Abukir. Jean Yves continued to work on terrestrial sites and moved offshore in the early 1990s with the study of the Pharos remains and finds of amphorae near Alexandria. At this time Franck Goddio obtained permission for his team to map the harbour and city remains east of the Pharos. With seed money provided by the Amoco Foundation, Cheryl Ward and Douglas Haldane of the Institute of Nautical Archaeology (INA) established in 1993 a 'branch office' in Egypt. In addition to organising a shipwreck survey in the Red Sea, they explored the pharaonic anchorage at Marsa Gawasis, medieval and early modern Quseir, Sadana Island, Hurgada and Ras Mohamed National Park in Sinai. They collaborated with the Supreme Council of Antiquities (SCA) of Egypt and their Underwater Archaeology section to establish a conservation laboratory and storage facility in Alexandria. Laboratory and conservation work continued under INA until 2002. Several Mediterranean coastal archaeological surveys were directed by Douglas Haldane and the excavation of the mid-18th century Sadana Island shipwreck was carried out by Cheryl Ward. Much of the funding came from generous corporate and individual sponsors and for operations from INA. The laboratory transferred to SCA and continues to process underwater finds from other projects although the INA-Egypt office closed in 2001. Many Egyptian students and archaeologists of SCA worked with Haldane and Ward over the years and have continued to be active in the field, including Professor Emad Khalil of the University of Alexandria. Haldane and Ward's intention was to build a partnership focused on scientific maritime archaeology. It was a great pleasure for Cheryl Ward to see that idea carried forward by the people they have had the privilege of working with.

27. How did maritime archaeology start in France?

Experts in England, France, the USA and other countries realised the importance of developing underwater archaeology and the need for archaeologists to undergo training in diving and exploration techniques. The French Government was the first to set up a research institute to undertake underwater archaeological research. In the year 1966, the Direction des Recherches Archeologiques Sous-Marine (DRASM) was created at Fort Saint Jean in Marseille under the Ministry of Culture. Subsequently DRASM was authorised to control the exploration of rivers and lakes and was renamed DRASSM. Two main factors contributed to the development of maritime archaeology in France: (i) French legislation on maritime wrecks. Under this legislation nobody may explore shipwrecks without permission; (ii) geographical location: France is bordered by the Mediterranean, Atlantic and the Channel. The main focus of DRASSM is maritime trade and shipwreck archaeology. Since 1960 more than 600 shipwrecks ranging from the 6th century BC to the end of the19th century AD have been catalogued by DRASSM. In addition to investigation of shipwrecks DRASSM has studied shipbuilding technology, dating by means of dendrochronology, and the study of amphorae to elucidate Classical trade and commerce. A number of post-medieval shipwrecks have been excavated; of importance were *Bateguier*, *Cavalaire*, *Lomellina*, *La Hougue*, *Slava Rossii* and *CSS Alabama*. Every year DRASSM publishes and brings out reports on the results of French underwater excavation.

28. How was maritime archaeology started in Greece?

Greece is rich in maritime archaeology and traditions. Christos Tsountas carried out the first underwater archaeological explorations between the islands of Salamis and Attica with the help of sponge divers in 1884. Subsequently, the sponge divers and fishermen of Greece found several masterpieces of art off the Greek coast. In 1960 Nikos Yialouris, a diving archaeologist carried out explorations at Pheia in the Peloponnese. More extensive maritime archaeological research, started in 1970 under his direction, led to the establishment of the Hellenic Institute of Marine Archaeology in 1973 and the Department of Underwater Antiquities in 1976. From 1980 onwards both organisations have undertaken underwater exploration and excavation of shipwrecks and submerged ports. Subsequently several other organisations have undertaken underwater exploration in Greece.

29. How was maritime archaeology started in Israel?

Maritime archaeology started in Israel in the middle of the 20th century. Its birthplace there was Caesarea. Elisha Linder and Raban Avner, especially, took an interest in nurturing this discipline in Israel. In 1960 the late Baron Edmond de Rothschild, the owner of the whole of Caesarea, established the first Mediterranean diving centre in the country and formed the association which was known as the 'Israel Association of Underwater Research'. The Association was founded with the generous help of the Recanati family, who continue to support the work to this day. Most of the archaeological researches of Israel were carried out at Caesarea. The Mediterranean coast of Israel has several underwater sites spread all the way from Rosh Hanikra at the border with Lebanon, to Ashkelon on the border with the Gaza strip containing archaeological remains of ancient ships and ports, including sunken cargoes and anchors of various types and ages.

30. How did maritime archaeology start in Italy?

Before the creation of a maritime archaeological research unit by the government, several excavations had been conducted by Italian archaeologists and other international organisations, such as INA of America, Oxford University MARE of the UK, the University of Haifa, Israel, together with individual scholars, such as Peter Throckmorton, Honor Frost, Gerhard Kapitan and A. J. Parker. Maritime archaeology in Italy has witnessed a significant development since 1980. After underwater archaeology was recognised by the Ministry of Culture in 1986 it provided assistance for maritime archaeological research programmes. Under Italy's current law any underwater find must be reported immediately to the relevant organisation and any individual may be granted permission to undertake excavation provided archaeological methodologies and rules are followed. Among important finds, the recovery of Caligula's pleasure barges from Lake Nemi; the retrieval of 11,000 wine amphorae from a Roman cargo ship wrecked at Albenga off the Ligurian coast and the discovery of numerous amphorae, anchor stocks, and Classical bronze statues are evidence of long distance maritime trade in the Mediterranean.

31. How did maritime archaeology start in Japan?

Although Japan is a country of islands and surrounded by the sea, marine archaeology was not active until recently. With the advancement of technology and development of skills more attention is now paid to underwater archaeology and academic research is growing. It is believed that Japanese maritime archaeology began in 1909 with the investigation of Lake Suwa, Nagano where earthenware and stone implements were collected. Professor Torao Mozai of Tokai University carried out underwater exploration at Takashima and a wide variety of Chinese wares, ornaments, armour, etc. were recovered. Shipwreck exploration began in 1974 to locate the 19th century warship *Kaiyou Maru* off the Gulf of Esahi, Hokkaido and used modern technology and traditional archaeological methods. In April 1977 off Kagawa a shipwreck was located in 20-40 m of water and the remains were documented. Similarly, in 1980-81 a Mongolian invasion ship was investigated off Tkashima and the timbers were recorded. The exploration of the Japanese *Iroha-maru* (1867) off Hiroshima at a depth of 27 m was successfully completed between 1988 and 1989. In 1980 a survey was conducted to locate the remains of Kublai Khan's fleet which was sunk by a typhoon in 1281in the Bay of Imari, Kyushu. The Asian Research Institute of Underwater Archaeology headed by Kenzou Hayashida has been active in recent years and is leading the project of the Museum of Underwater Cultural Heritage. Attempts have been made to locate the islands which sank in the earthquakes of 1026 and 1956. Since 1972 underwater investigation and geophysical surveys have been carried out off the Yonaguni and Chatan islands. Exploration has yielded remains of stone masonry buildings, roads with water channels and retaining walls. It is believed that these could be between 5,000 and 1,500 years old, while the remains lying in deeper water may be much older. As part of international technical support, Japan salvaged artefacts in Iraq in 1971-1972. In 1985 international cooperation in the excavation of sunken ships was carried out in Syria. In recent years, academic exchange has taken place with the neighbouring countries of China, Korea and Australia.

32. How did maritime archaeology start in Malaysia?

The Department of Museums and Antiquities of the Ministry of Culture of Malaysia established the Maritime Archaeological Museum in 2001. Its objectives are: to collect information related to maritime activities; to undertake underwater survey and excavation; to create public awareness; and to preserve and exhibit finds. Nanhai Maritime Archaeology has surveyed several shipwrecks in Malaysian waters, namely, *Tanjung Simpang Mengayau* (960-1279 CE), *Wanli* (1630), *Diana* (1817) and *Desaru* (1830). In the course of exploration Song Dynasty ceramics were collected from the *Tanjung Simpang Mengayau* site. The *Wanli* wreck was loaded with *Kraak* and other porcelain wares. It appears that the ship was built either in India or the Philippines and the second layer of hull planks were from China. The ship's anchor, iron cannon, coins, blue and white porcelain from the Jingdezhen kiln, Yixing ware, spoons and stoneware jars were found in the *Desaru* shipwreck. The ship *Diana* was sailed for India in 1817 and was wrecked after striking submerged boulders in the Straits of Malacca. Blue and white porcelain, glass bottles and other artefacts were recovered from the site. Apart from these wrecks, in 1985 the Dutch East India Company fluit *Risdam* was explored off Mersing in association with Negara Museum.

33. How was underwater archaeology started in the Netherlands?

Underwater archaeology in the Netherlands was developed late. Some initiatives were undertaken to carry out research in Dutch rivers and in the sea off the Netherlands in the early 1960s. They aimed at submerged sites of the Roman period. These initiatives, however, were not consolidated and thus, when in 1970 the National Museum of Antiquities was confronted with the discovery of the displaced and submerged Roman sanctuary dedicated to the goddess *Nehalennia*, there were no archaeologists cum divers to deploy for the purpose. In the late 1970s the situation changed when the Minister of Culture took the initiative for three major reasons. First, there was a growing number of finds collected by recreational divers, but as there was no institute to take care of the findings a number of artefacts were lost due to lack of conservation. Secondly, a number of wrecks belonging to the Dutch East India Company (VOC) were discovered elsewhere in the world. Thirdly, the parliamentary assembly of the Council of Europe recommended proper initiatives in this regard. Subsequently, a committee was constituted and a part-time researcher was appointed to make an inventory of problems and to develop a policy. As a result of this, the '*Afdeling Archeologie Onder water*' (AAO) came into existence. AAO started archaeological research in Dutch waters and collaborated with the established archaeological institutions working on land. In 1998, AAO was merged with the organisation involved in ship archaeological research and the new institute came into the lime light. Known as the Netherlands Institute for Ship and Underwater Archaeology (NISA), it functioned under the aegis of the State Service for Archaeological Investigations. In 2006 the national services for architectural and archaeological heritage were integrated into the Netherlands Department for the Preservation of Archaeological Heritage, Cultural Landscapes and Historic Buildings (RACM). This integration was coincidental with a major reshuffling of the organization of archaeology. The department is responsible for policies and guidelines. Other institutions are now contributing for the growth underwater archaeology as well.

34. How did maritime archaeology start in Portugal?

Before maritime archaeological research began, artefacts such as amphorae had been reported by dredging and fishing industries operating in the Arade, Sado and Tagus rivers. Timbers from medieval shipbuilding were found on the south side of Lisbon, a few hundred metres inland from the present waterfront on the River Tagus. In 1988 the first underwater exploration in Portugal took place along the coast of Peniche, north of Lisbon to locate the remains of the Spanish warship *San Pedro de Alcantata* (1786). However, commercial exploration of the Portuguese underwater heritage was promoted in the last decades of the 20th century. The then director of the National Museum of Archaeology, Francisco J. S. Alves, played a leading role in the administration and the general election of 1995 brought about a drastic change of policy. That year, in order to preserve underwater sites, the National Center for Nautical and Underwater Archaeology (CNANS) was established in Lisbon as part of the Portuguese Institute of Archaeology (IPA). The main objective of CNANS is to promote underwater archaeology for purely scientific purposes. Under this programme the Center has been collecting information on Portuguese ships lost all over the world, collating archaeological information and written documents. In addition it has surveyed and excavated several shipwrecks in Portuguese waters. Among others, the important shipwrecks of *Nossa Senhora dos Martires* (1606) and the 15th century *Ria de Aveiro* wreck have been excavated on the bar of the River Tagus and in the Aveiro lagoon respectively. CNANS has an agreement of mutual co-operation with NAS.

35. How did maritime archaeology begin in Scotland?

Scotland has a long coastline and many ships from Europe sailed north around its rocky coast rather than through the narrow English channel. So it is rich in wrecks, which still attract treasure hunters. Several Dutch East Indiamen, for example, have been salvaged, notably from Shetland e.g. *Lastdrager* 1654 and De *Liefde* (1711). An era began in the maritime archaeology of Scotland with the establishment of research institute at the University of St. Andrews in 1973 for fostering and developing maritime archaeology. Later this provided a base for the archaeological diving unit, covering the whole of the United Kingdom. The successor of this unit is now based in England, but Scotland still leads the way in concern about the maritime cultural heritage, and there is a dedicated inspector within the National Heritage Agency Historic Scotland. Since then the maritime archaeology is on the forefront and has an archaeology diving unit of its own. Afterwards exploration of several shipwrecks were carried out among them the important ones were *Kennemerland* 1664, *Dartmouth* 1690 and *Swan* 1653. *Kennemerland* wrecked after striking the outcrop of rock close to the mouth of the natural harbour of the Out Skerries in Shetland. It was through excavating this scattered wreck that Keith Muckelroy developed his theories about scattered wreck sites. *Dartmouth* was built in 1655 and wrecked in a gale on 6 October 1690 in the Sound of Mull off the west coast of Scotland. Salvage carried out soon after the wreck, but again it was located by a group of divers from Bristol. The subsequent exploration yielded three types of cast iron guns, ship's bell with date, pistol, a musket stock, various types of pottery, glass bottles, clay pipes, etc. The English warship *Swan* 1653 was wrecked in the Sound of Mull thirty seven years before the loss of *Dartmouth*. The *Dartmouth* timbers, for example, yielded useful information about 17th century shipbuilding.

36. How did maritime archaeology start in Sweden?

Salvage operations on sunken ships were executed in Sweden in the 16th and 17th centuries by professional state sponsored companies. For example, guns were raised from the warship *Vasa* (1628) in the 1660s and from *Kronan* (1676) in the 1680s. Early underwater investigations with more scientific and archaeological motives were carried out in the 1920s by Admiral Carl Ekman on the sunken warship *Elefanten* (1565). During the same period another military man, Axel Zetterling, was involved in the investigation of a Viking Age sunken wooden castle called 'Balverket' in Lake Tingstäde on the island of Gotland. The royal warship *Vasa* was found by engineer Anders Franzen in 1956. Modern maritime archaeology in Sweden started after the raising of the *Vasa* in 1961. The cold brackish water of the Baltic Sea preserves wooden ships in a unique way and in the 1970s the Swedish National Maritime Museum of Stockholm carried out several pilot excavations on shipwrecks, for example, the *Jutholmen* (1700) and 18th century *Ālvsnabben*. In the early 1980s the excavation of the warship *Kronan* by Kalmar County Museum started as a project and is still is on-going in 2008. New investigations took place on 'Balverket' in Lake Tingstäde in the 1990s. Most maritime archaeological investigation projects in Sweden are today run by the Stockholm Maritime Museum and its special unit for contract archaeology. Academic training and research in maritime archaeology are performed by Sodertorn University College. The majority of investigations focus on well preserved shipwrecks. In 2007, for example, an almost fully intact '*flute*' from the middle of the 17th century was found. In addition other sources of information are investigated today, for example, the harbour of the Viking Age town of Birka and the underwater landscape of the maritime city of Stockholm.

37. How was maritime archaeology introduced in South Africa?

In 1988, the University of Cape Town introduced maritime archaeology as a scientific specialisation in South Africa. After a lengthy procedure, Dutch maritime archaeologist and historian Dr Bruno Werz was put in charge and several national projects were undertaken. These include a survey of shipwrecks around the infamous Robben Island; the excavation of a well in Cape Town Castle; the underwater excavation of two Dutch East India Company ships in Table Bay and Operation *Zembe* ('Axe'). This last project was initiated in 2002, after the discovery of the world's oldest underwater artefacts in Table Bay.

Although these projects were very successful, financial constraints hampered further development of the field. After some years Dr Werz left the university and continued with his work as Director of the Southern African Institute of Maritime Archaeology (SAIMA). At present, the SAIMA plays a leading role in further research along the southern African coast. Besides a considerable output as far as scientific literature is concerned, maritime archaeology has enjoyed considerable media coverage. Several television documentaries were produced, not to mention hundreds of articles in the popular media, both in South Africa as well as overseas. Although the specialization has not yet reached its full potential, it looks as if maritime archaeology in South Africa has a bright future.

38. How did maritime archaeology start in Soviet Union/Russia?

In Russia maritime archaeology developed in four stages from its emergence in the 18th century to the implementation of scientific methodology in 1990. In most instances underwater exploration in Russia has been initiated by museums bordering the Black Sea to locate the submerged ancient towns of Dioscuria (1876), Feodosiya (1905) and Olbia (1909). Professor R. A. Orbeli has carried out exploration at Feodosiya, Chersonese and at Olbia and has recorded log boats of the 1st millennium BC. Orbeli has initiated and formulated objectives for maritime archaeological research and developed scientific approaches. Similarly, in 1957-8 Professor V. D. Blavatski investigated the submerged town of Thanagoria and mapped its layout, and in 1961 examined the submerged structures of Olbia using geoacoustics, and explored several shipwrecks. Between 1986 and 1990 several submerged settlements were surveyed in the Black Sea, the most significant being ancient Akra and Korokondama. After the formation of Russia in 1990 the Centre for Complex Underwater Studies of the Scientific and Research Institute of Culture was founded and since 1990 among other activities of the Centre has explored the significant submerged settlement of Patrei.

39. How did maritime archaeology start in Sri Lanka?

The National Aquatic Resources Agency (NARA) of Sri Lanka was established in 1982 in order to check treasure hunting. The primary objectives of NARA were to preserve and safeguard biological and mineral resources and marine archaeological sites. The Director of Merchant Shipping often consulted NARA on the issue of licenses for wreck salvage and determination of the historical significance of a shipwreck. In this connection an international seminar on marine archaeology was organised and scholars from various disciplines participated. In 1986 P. U. Weerawardena presented a paper on the maritime history of Sri Lanka at the First National Archaeological Congress and this generated interest among scholars. Again, in 1988 the Maritime Heritage Trust of Sri Lanka organised a seminar on maritime archaeology and participants included Arthur C. Clarke and Mike Wilson, who had collected sacks of silver coins minted in Surat from the Great Basses Reef. Following this the government brought in legislation and approved the setting up of a Maritime Cultural Heritage Authority. The Galle Harbour Project commenced in 1992 and was coordinated by Jeremy Green of AIMA, Australia, and Somasiri Devendra of Sri Lanka with the objective of training youngsters in maritime archaeology, diving, conservation and the compilation of shipwreck databases. Along with training under water, surveys were carried out and two Dutch East Indianman wrecks, the *Hercules* and the *Avondster*, were explored and the Project continued until 1998. Shipwrecks and remains of human habitation known to be lying under water off Sri Lanka are yet to be investigated.

40. How was maritime archaeology started in the UK?

After returning from Cape Gelidonya, Joan du Plat Taylor laid the foundations of this discipline in Britain in 1961. As the librarian of the Institute of Archaeology, London and she promoted the activities from that base until her death. It was she who realized that maritime archaeology should not fall into wrong hands and therefore she made constant efforts to educate a number of sports divers about the importance of underwater heritage. Fortunately, in UK the sport diving organisation, the British Sub-Aqua club, already existed and this assisted Joan du Plat Taylor in promoting maritime archaeology there. Subsequently, she formed the Council for Nautical Archaeology (CNA) with representatives of various universities, museums and institutes. She realised that in order to be recognised as an academic discipline, an academic journal as a forum for scholars was essential and founded the International Journal of Nautical Archaeology (IJNA).

41. How was maritime archaeology started in the USA?

From the early 1960s a classical archaeologist, George F. Bass, who was working on ancient shipwrecks in the Mediterranean Sea, provided motivation and opportunities to students for the development of maritime archaeology. The National Park Service, which is the primary historic preservation agency in the USA, carried out several underwater surveys by archaeologists from 1968 onwards. Prior to this some societies and institutes had conducted underwater explorations. For example, the Peabody Museum sponsored the excavation of the Chichen Itza cenote (sacred well) in Mexico as early as 1905. From 1973 onwards the Institute of Nautical Archaeology (INA) has served as the main instrument for promoting maritime archaeology. Maritime archaeological sites in America were found in the sea and in fresh water, and the extensive coastline also contributed to the resource base for underwater archaeological research.

In the United States, the salvage of treasure from shipwrecks by commercial divers led to a law giving protection of shipwrecks to the individual states in whose waters the wrecks lie; hence some states have imposed legal controls on underwater sites and some states have established underwater archaeological units. In recent years the exploration and excavation of prehistoric vessels, submerged sites and shipwrecks have been undertaken by these states and are of great quality and high standard.

CHAPTER TWO

MARITIME HISTORY AND BEGINNING OF MARITIME ARCHAEOLOGY IN INDIA

1. How old is the maritime history of India and its overseas contacts?

India's contribution to the ancient maritime tradition of the world, in terms of development of ports and harbour engineering, shipbuilding and navigation technology, trade and commerce is very significant. It is an established fact that seafaring in India is as old as its civilization (about 5000 years) and India is one of the oldest maritime nations of the world. Contacts of the Indus civilisation with Egypt and Mesopotamia in the third millennium BC have been documented. Roman, Greek and Southeast Asian maritime trade with India flourished from the beginning of the Christian era. Similarly, the Kalingas and the Cholas occupied a prominent role in maritime trade between India and Southeast Asia. Before the arrival of the Europeans, the Arabs and the Chinese controlled the Indian Ocean for centuries. However, great impetus was given to maritime expeditions during the early 16th century AD. Portuguese, British, Dutch, French and Danish explored the sea routes to India in search of spices and at last landed in India via Africa and Madagascar. Subsequently, these Europeans established trade centres and colonies. Afterwards they occupied Indian territories and ruled India till the 20th century.

2. What Indian evidences were found in overseas countries and vice versa?

Harappan type seals, stone weights, long etched carnelian beads, beads made of semiprecious stone, black and red pottery, bronze objects have been found variously in excavations at Bahrain, Failaka and Oman in the Arabian Peninsula and at Ur, Kish and Brak in Iraq and Hissar and Susa in Iran. Similarly, a number of seals, beads and dice resembling the Harappan type have been recovered from Mesopotamia. Socotara, at the mouth of the Red Sea, was an important entrepot for exchanging Indian goods from Harappan time onwards. The occurrence of Harappan chessmen in the tomb of the Egyptian Queen Hatshepsut is a clear indication of extensive overseas trade of India during the 3rd millennium BC. The terracotta figures of a gorilla and a mummy from Lothal likewise show overseas contact with Egypt. The presence of circular seals bearing Indus script and motifs in the Persian Gulf and cylinder seals bearing similar motifs and scripts in the Euphrates and Tigris valley indicates that Indians had established their colonies in Mesopotamia and Bahrain.

3. Which were the Harappan period ports and trade centres of India and what archaeological evidence was found from these ports?

The Harappan period ports and trade centres of India were Lothal, Kuntasi, Dholavira, Megham, Nageswar, Bet Dwarka, Padri, Lakhabaval, Todio and Prabhas-Somnath, all in Gujarat on the west coast of India. The earliest dock of India has been unearthed at Lothal. This trapezoidal basin measured 214 x 36 m, was enclosed by kiln-fired brick walls with sluice gates that enabled ships at high tide to enter through an inlet channel which was 12 m wide. A mud brick platform was built adjoining the northern wall of the dockyard to serve as a wharf. Stone anchors have also been recovered.

The excavations at Prabhas-Somnath brought to light a warehouse close to the river Hiranya, which is similar to the warehouse of Tepe Yahya in West Asia. The findings of Bet Dwarka encompass a Harappan type seal, graffiti on potsherds, a copper fish hook, terracotta and fish bone beads and shell bangles belonging to the late Harappan period. A landing platform made of mud mortar and flat stone blocks has been excavated at Kuntasi that was meant for loading and unloading cargo. A slope was provided for facilitating the handling of cargo. Kuntasi has also yielded three stone anchors. Similarly, the excavations at Inamgaon, Maharashtra revealed a jetty having a slope towards the river that served as a landing platform, although a major portion of the jetty has been washed out owing to frequent floods. Besides structural remains from these port sites, the other finds include various types of seals and sealing, stone anchors, terracotta artefacts and varieties of beads that indicate India's overseas contacts.

4. What is a port and where are some important ancient ports of India?

The word 'port' is derived from the Latin word '*Portus*' meaning gateway. Thus a port can be defined as a gate or entrance from the sea to land or land to sea. The ancient Indian architectural text '*Silpasastras*' mentions two types of ports namely 'Pattana' and 'Dronimukhi'. A pattana was situated on the sea coast where ships were loaded and unloaded as well as anchored, whereas a dronimukhi was situated near the meeting place of river and sea. Along the 7516 km long coastline of India, several ports and trade centres existed. Among them a few important ports were Tamralipti, Chandraketugarh, Manikpatna, Palur, Kalingapatnam, Dantapur, Dharanikota, Kotapatnam, Arikamedu, Poompuhar, Alagankulam, Muziris, Sopara and Barygaza. The geomorphological features of the coastline of India were favourable for establishing a number of ports. Archaeological, literary, epigraphical evidence; foreign accounts; and other sources confirm this fact. The ports of India had hinterland connections by riverine and caravan trade routes.

5. What features are generally found at port sites?

Discoveries at port and harbour sites include boatbuilding yards, anchors, landing places, dockyards, causeways, wharves, jetties, embankments, breakwaters, warehouses and moorings on the sea front. The recent archaeological explorations and excavations along the coast of India have brought to light the existence of wharves, warehouses, jetties, anchoring places, stone and iron anchors and lighthouses at Dharanikota, Kotapatnam (AP), Arikamedu (Pondicherry), Kaveripattinam and Mahabalipuram (Tamil Nadu), Udayavara (Karnataka), Ganjam and Chilika (Orissa), Lothal, Kuntasi and Prabhas Somnath (Gujarat) and Inamgaon (Maharashtra). Varieties of stone anchors have been found at various port sites including Minicoy Island of Lakshadweep, India.

6. Have underwater explorations been carried out at any port sites of India?

Yes, underwater exploration and excavation have been carried out at Dwarka, Bet Dwarka, Somnath, Vijaydurg, Mahabalipuram and Poompuhar which were the ancient ports of India. Varieties of stone and iron anchors, pottery and stone and brick structures were noticed during explorations. Besides excavations, onshore surveys have been conducted at other port sites of

Maharashtra, Orissa, Andhra Pradesh, Gujarat, Karnataka and Tamil Nadu; the causes of their decline have been studied. Stone anchors reported from some sites shed new light on their contacts with other ports of India and abroad.

7. What is a harbour and what are the differences between port and harbour?

A 'harbour' can be defined as a sheltered area in or near the sea where vessels could be launched, built or taken for repair, or could seek refuge in bad weather, or to provide facilities for loading and unloading of cargo and passengers. Thus, the term port is used to indicate a harbour where additional facilities such as a warehouse, landing of passengers and cargo are provided. In general it can be stated that a port includes a harbour or in other words every port is a harbour but the reverse is not the fact.

8. What is an anchor and its importance in maritime archaeological studies?

In simple terms an anchor denotes a mechanical device that prevents a vessel from moving. Anchors are required for every vessel, from small craft to modern container ships and oil carriers. In earlier days watercraft were anchored in lakes, rivers and the sea by deploying a stone of required size tied rope, or a stone bound to a hook shaped wooden element. These stone anchors show the intensity of trade, sizes of ships, maritime contacts and their provenance. In India, categories of stone anchors have been reported from Gujarat, Maharashtra, Goa, Kerala, Lakshadweep, Tamil Nadu and Orissa. In India the evolution and development of stone anchors have been studied, leading to the classification of anchors on the basis of their shape, type and provenance. Comparative study of stone anchors from India has been made with finds from Sri Lanka, the Persian Gulf and the Mediterranean Sea.

9. What types of stone anchors have been found in Indian waters?

Varieties of stone anchors such as composite (triangular), Indo-Arabian (grapnel) and ring stone (mushroom) single hole types have been reported from the intertidal zone, onshore and underwater explorations of India (Fig. 2). Land excavations at Lothal and Kuntasi have brought to light simplest type of stone anchors. These do not resemble other stone anchors which have been found during maritime archaeological explorations. The anchors of Lothal and Kuntasi

Fig. 2 Various types of stone anchors recovered from Indian waters

have been dated in context with archaeological findings (3500-1700 BC) whereas anchors found during maritime archaeological explorations have been dated on a comparative basis between the early historical period and the 20th century AD. Composite stone anchors have been reported only from the port sites of Gujarat and Maharashtra, whereas Indo-Arabian stone anchors have been found at Minicoy, Kerala, Tamil Nadu and Goa including Gujarat and Maharashtra. Recent explorations at Chilika Lake, Orissa and the Manapad region of Tamil Nadu have yielded single hole stone anchors.

10. What are the evidence of use of sails in Indian ships?

Unlike anchors, sails also play a vital role in maritime trade. The Harappan square seal with perforated boss depicts a ship with a big sail hoisted near the raked prow. Ships of ancient period could set sail during the favourable wind hence the voyages were necessarily seasonal and ships would have used either square or lateen sails. Sails have been depicted on the boats of Ajanta cave paintings, but those are datable to 6th century AD.

The Punch-marked coins with ship motifs have been reported from Wari-Bateshwar and Narsingdi in Bangladesh. Ship graffiti on a potsherd which appears like Roman sailing vessel with masts has been recovered from Alagankulam, Tamil Nadu. The Satavahana (2nd century BC to 3rd century AD), Salankayana (AD 300-440) Kurumbas and Pallava (6th to 9th century AD) coins depict ships with masts. Similarly, the terracotta seals from Bangarh, Chandraketugarh and Tamralipti depict seagoing vessels. All these finds depict ships but sails are depicted along with masts are not clear.

11. What kinds of boats were used by Indian mariners and how did they sail?

The representation of boats on seals, coins and potsherds confirms that strong seafaring activity prevailed from Harappan times. The boats used by the Harappans were flat bottomed with a sharp upturned prow and stern (Fig. 3a). Evidence of shipbuilding and navigation is available in abundance after the early historical period. The types of rafts and boats used in the Indian subcontinent are mentioned by their names from the 1st century AD onwards, but their structural details, methods of propulsion and other details are scarcely noted. In any coastal environment the nature of sea craft is conditioned by the physical characteristics of the coastline and racial history of the seafaring community.

3a

3b

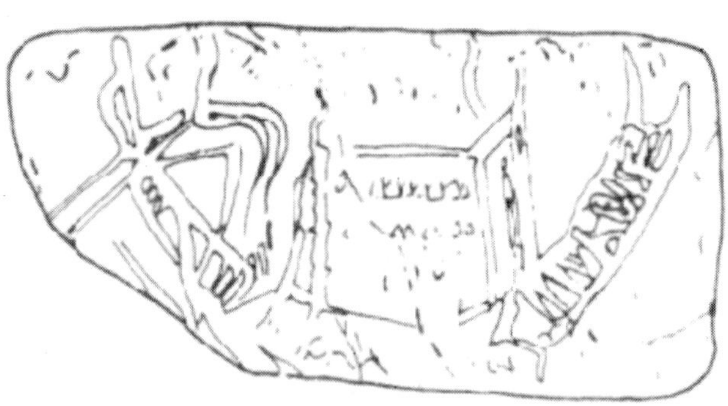

Fig. 3a & 3b Boats depicted on Harappa and Mohenjodaro seals

Various types of boats and ships used in rivers and the sea for transporting cargo, passengers and necessities of warfare are represented on the walls of the temples of West Bengal, Orissa, Tamil Nadu, Karnataka and Rajasthan, Buddhist caves and stupas of Maharashtra, Orissa and Madhya Pradesh, rock paintings in Gujarat and hero stones of Goa.

In ancient times Indian sailors possessed precise astronomical knowledge and they navigated with an approximation in relation to the sun's azimuth or the stars according to time and season. The position of the ship was estimated from its average speed on the basis of experience and velocity of wind or the prevailing conditions of the sea. Tamed birds '*Disha Kaka*' were kept on deck as land finders to indicate the coast. '*Disha Kaka*' are also seen on Mohenjodaro seals (Fig. 3b). Ancient texts emphasise the skill of the pilots and their experience of the conditions of the sea and the changes in the behaviour of wind. Rectangular and lateen types of sails have been used by Indians since Harappan times.

12. What are the prospects for maritime archaeology in India?

From the Harappan period onwards several ports and trade centres existed along the 7516 km long coastline of India. Available archaeological and literary evidence indicates that ports and trade centres declined due to both manmade and natural factors. Some of the ports and trade centres have been identified, whereas some are mentioned in literature but so far not located due to lack of substantial evidence. Similarly, a number of ships which have been wrecked in Indian waters need to be explored. Students and scholars can undertake various kinds of research on maritime archaeology as their Ph. D. programmes, while researchers and college and university teachers can pursue research in this field (even without undertaking underwater exploration). Some of the subjects related to maritime archaeology can be introduced in school and college curricula in India. There is a wide scope for further research in this discipline.

13. What was the status of maritime archaeology before its beginning in India?

Before the beginning of marine archaeological studies at NIO in 1981 as a project, the Department of Archaeology, Government of Tamil Nadu had approached to NIO to undertake offshore explorations of Poompuhar to locate any the submerged habitational remains of the port of Kaveripatnam. Accordingly, scientists of NIO, namely K. H. Vora and L. V. Subbaraju conducted a geophysical survey off Poompuhar in 1981 and recorded some conspicuous features such as peaks and pinnacles of 2 to 5 m height in echograms, and geometric shapes on sonograms in 18 to 19 m water depth. The results of the offshore survey suggested that those features could be submerged habitational structures or shipwrecks. Subsequent underwater explorations off Poompuhar yielded submerged structures and a shipwreck.

14. Who founded maritime archaeological studies in India?

S. R. Rao (Shikaripur Ranganatha Rao, b. 1922) was the founder of maritime archaeological studies in India at NIO, Goa in 1981 after his retirement from the Archaeological Survey of India (ASI). The projects he dealt with were submerged Dwarka on the Gujarat coast and Poompuhar, the submerged port town of early Chola Period on the Tamil Nadu coast.

In addition to Dwarka and Poompuhar, Dr Rao undertook underwater explorations and coastal surveys at Bet Dwarka, Somnath, Goa and Lakshadweep on the west coast and Tranquebar on the east coast of India. He also carried out onshore explorations along the coast of Tamil Nadu, Orissa and Maharashtra. Dr Rao has put India on the maritime archaeological map of the world. To promote maritime archaeology on India he founded the Society for Marine Archaeology (SMA) at NIO and organised several conferences and seminars on maritime archaeology of India and the Indian Ocean countries. Dr Rao left NIO in 1997 after his active involvement in underwater explorations of India ceased.

15. What aspects inspired Dr Rao to establish maritime archaeological studies in India?

In Gujarat the findings of Lothal excavations (Rao 1973) provided evidence for overseas trade contacts of India with Bahrain, Egypt, Failaka, Mesopotamia and Oman in the third millennium BC. This was possible because of the berthing facilities provided by the construction of the first tidal dock in the world at Lothal. Maritime trade has been continuing for the last 5000 years or so and there were inevitably shipwrecks during this time. During his tenure at the Archaeological Survey of India (ASI) Dr Rao had carried out extensive exploration and excavation at several protohistoric and early historic sites and observed that several port towns of India had been submerged.

During visits abroad he had met Sir Mortimer Wheeler, George F. Bass, Alexander Flinder, Joan du Plat Taylor, Valerie Fenwick and many others who were undertaking shipwreck studies in Mediterranean waters. Dr Rao was fascinated by this discipline and thought of starting this discipline in India. He took keen interest in this subject and gathered information on its procedures, acquired equipment, and appointed archaeologists and diver photographers for underwater exploration and photography. After his retirement from ASI, with financial support from the Government of India he led the first underwater explorations in 1981-82 off Dwarka on the west coast of India. He believed that if underwater explorations were carried out in Indian waters remains of the cultural heritage might come to light which were not known hitherto. During the same time maritime archaeology was also an upcoming subject throughout the world.

16. How and when did maritime archaeological explorations start in India?

In India, maritime archaeological research was initiated in 1981 by establishment of the Marine Archaeology Unit (MAU) in the National Institute of Oceanography (NIO), Goa with financial assistance from the Indian National Science Academy (INSA) to undertake studies off Dwarka. Subsequently, the Department of Science and Technology (DST), funded exploration off Dwarka. The Archaeological Survey of India funded training of manpower in diving and underwater explorations off Dwarka, Bet Dwarka and Somnath and the Department of Ocean Development (DOD) funded projects for undertaking exploration of shipwrecks on the west coast of India and explorations off Dwarka, Bet Dwarka and Somnath. In the year 1990 the Marine Archaeology Unit became an integral part of the NIO and is now known as Marine Archaeology Centre (MAC). The emergence of maritime archaeology has added a new chapter to Indian oceanographic studies. Though maritime archaeology developed late, it has made excellent progress and is a fast developing discipline in India. The centre at NIO, Goa is foremost in maritime archaeological studies in India.

17. What are the capabilities and equipment NIO possesses for maritime archaeological research?

Presently, the Marine Archaeology Centre of NIO has a well experienced team of archaeologists able to dive to 30 m water depth and to carry out underwater archaeological exploration. In addition to diving gear and diving personnel, the centre possesses an underwater communication system, metal detectors, underwater still and video cameras, a remotely operated vehicle, compressors, etc. Besides, these scientific tools, new methods are being deployed to carry out underwater searches. In short, the centre is self equipped for undertaking all kinds of underwater exploration in shallow waters. The team has been engaged in the

R&D activities of the NIO and involved in Environmental Impact Assessment (EIA) studies for developing industries along the coast and offshore region of India.

18. What are the other institutes and organisations undertaking maritime archaeological studies in India?

The University Grants Commission (UGC) established the Centre for Underwater Archaeology, at Tamil University, Thanjavur, Tamil Nadu in 1983. However, the centre has concentrated more on traditional navigation and shipbuilding technology of peninsular India and the Lakshadweep, Andaman and Nicobar Islands. The centre has also retrieved stone and iron anchors from the Tamil Nadu coast. The Marine Archaeology Centre of Andhra University, Visakhapatnam has carried out underwater explorations off the Visakhapatnam coast to locate the remains of the submerged Shiva temple of the 10th-11th centuries AD. In the recent past the Archaeological Survey of India has set up the Marine Archaeology Wing and undertaken surveys off Lakshadweep and Mahabalipuram. Similarly, the National Institute of Ocean and Technology (NIOT), Chennai is also taking an interest in marine archaeology and has carried out geophysical surveys off the Gulf of Cambay, Gujarat. The Maritime History Society, Mumbai, of the Indian Navy every year conducts conferences and lecture programmes on the maritime archaeology in India.

19. What are the achievements of maritime archaeology in India?

In a span of more than two decades, NIO has undertaken offshore surveys to locate the remains of submerged ports and shipwrecks off Dwarka, Bet Dwarka, Somnath, Goa, Vijaydurg, Miyani, Visawada, Mahabalipuram, Lakshadweep, Poompuhar, Tranquebar and Manapad (Fig.1). Furthermore, onshore explorations have also been carried out along Andhra Pradesh, Gujarat, Karnataka, Kerala, Maharashtra, Orissa and the Tamil Nadu coast to trace the remains of maritime activities of India. Studies of traditional boatbuilding techniques have been recorded along the coast of Orissa and Karnataka. Recently, the Centre collaborated with the Scientific Exploration Society, UK to carry out studies off Dwarka, Poompuhar and Mahabalipuram. To disseminate maritime archaeological discoveries in Indian waters to the world two brief films were produced for ARD First German TV Network South Asia Studio and the ZDT TV (Second German Television) of Germany. Attempts have been made to study the sea level changes, coastal erosion and accretion along the Indian coast through maritime archaeological studies.

20. What are the results of maritime archaeological studies in India and their importance?

Onshore and offshore exploration and excavation artefacts from various sites of India include varieties of anchors, coins, guns, beads, terracotta ring wells, types of pottery, ingots, seals, structures and other artefacts which confirm that India had a rich cultural heritage that is now submerged. These artefacts attest that India had trade and cultural contacts with other countries from the 3rd-4th millennium BC onwards. Further, they prove that natural phenomena such as sea level changes, coastal erosion and accretion played a major role in destroying many ports and coastal habitational sites of India. The shipwreck exploration discoveries show the trade relations of India with other countries and the factors that caused the shipwrecks. Comprehensive information on all sites of India where maritime archaeological exploration has been carried out is provided elsewhere in the book (See Pages: 128-142).

21. What are the areas of marine archaeology which need to be developed in India?

The maritime history of India is more than 5000 years old. Since its beginning the Indian coast has witnessed trade, cultural and social contacts, with Egypt, Mesopotamia, Rome, Greece, Southeast Asian countries and the Arab world. In later periods, the Portuguese, Dutch, Danish, French and British came to India for the purpose of maritime trade and subsequently, conquered India and ruled till the 20th century. India had a number of ports and trade centres from the earliest times and those declined due to both natural and manmade causes. Some of the ports and trade centres have been identified by exploration and excavation; some have not been located, for various reasons. Over time innumerable Indian and foreign boats and ships have sunk in Indian waters. A few shipwrecks have been explored and other wrecks await the airlift of maritime archaeologists. The study of submerged and deserted ports and shipwrecks will provide a proper chronology and enhance our knowledge of the maritime history of India. Onshore, underwater and shipwreck exploration will help us to understand contacts between India and other countries, nature of trade and commerce, causes of shipwrecks and provenance of finds. Studies of ports will help to explain contacts with the hinterland and with other countries, and the causes of the ports' decline. In all, the artefacts and data would help to reconstruct the maritime history of India.

22. What is the general awareness of maritime archaeology in India?

General awareness of maritime archaeology and underwater cultural heritage in India is lacking among the ordinary people and needs to be enhanced as soon as possible. Maritime archaeology is perceived to be a very skilled and specialised subject. Similarly, in India diving is known only to a very limited number of people and an awareness drive on diving and underwater exploration is imperative among the scholars involved in this research. Further, this nascent discipline should be introduced in school and college syllabi, and public lectures and posters should be delivered and displayed all over India. Above all, for the progress and better prospects of this discipline proper initiatives should be taken by Government as well as concerned authorities at every stage.

23. What are the present apprehensions about maritime archaeological sites of India?

As a part of globalisation varieties of new industries and constructions are evolving and developments are taking place along the coastal belt as well as in the nearshore and offshore region of India. These activities may destroy forever the evidence of a bygone civilisation which has been neither located nor explored. In view of this it is highly imperative for maritime archaeologists to undertake coastal and offshore exploration and demarcate endangered areas before any further destruction takes place. Each discovery has some importance which cannot be ignored because it may shed new light on the maritime archaeology of India. Once the evidence is lost it can never be retrieved. For this reason it should be protected for the coming generations and studied in detail.

CHAPTER THREE

SOURCES AND OBJECTIVES OF MARITIME ARCHAEOLOGY

1. What are the sources for the study of maritime archaeology in India?

The sources for studies on maritime trade, ports, shipwrecks, cultural contacts of India can be classified into the following:

(a) Literary sources: epics such as *Mahabharata, Ramayana, Puranas, Buddhist Jatakas, Milindapanho, Sangam Texts, Tilakamanjari, Yuktikalpataru*, regional literature, palm leaf manuscripts, etc.

(b) Travellers accounts: *Periplus of the Erythaean Sea (Periplus Maris Erythraei), Pliny's Natural History*, Ptolemy's *Geography*, *Strabo's Geography*, Megasthene, Fa-Hien, Hiuen Tsang, Al-Biruni, Al-Masudi, Marco Polo, Ludovico Varthema, etc.

(c) Inscriptions and coins: Early Brahmi and Kharosthi inscriptions, Motupalli pillar inscription, old Balinese inscriptions of Semibiran and Indonesian inscriptions, punch mark coins, Roman and Greek coins, etc.

(d) Archaeological artefacts such as various types of pottery, graffiti on pottery, amphorae, etc.

(e) Paper record: Archival records and documents pertaining to shipping, maritime trade, charts and maps, maritime casualties which are housed in archives, libraries and private collections in India and abroad.

(f) Information from local fishermen, scholars, folklore, traditional knowledge and legends.

2. Have any sites of India been explored based on the descriptions given in literature?

Yes, the Sangam period (3rd century BC to 3rd century AD) texts such as *Manimekhalai* and *Cilappatikaram* mention that Poompuhar, the early Chola capital and wealthy river port along the Tamil Nadu coast is said to have been submerged in the sea. The text mentions that the Chola king had lost his son and in grief the king forgot to celebrate the annual festival of Lord Indra. This enraged the goddess Manimekhalai who caused the city to be swallowed by the sea. Based on the descriptions extensive underwater explorations were carried out and a number of brick and stone structures and pottery were found both in near shore and offshore Poompuhar and adjoining regions (Fig. 4).

Fig. 4 Remains of a brick structure and terracotta ringwell found in the intertidal zone of Poompuhar, Tamil Nadu

3. **How are the findings correlated with the descriptions given in literature?**

As mentioned earlier, the Sangam texts *Manimekhalai* and *Cilappatikaram* state that Poompuhar (Kaveripatnam) had Roman colonies, Buddhist settlements, a water reservoir, market streets, wharfs, etc. Land excavations, and near shore and offshore surveys have unearthed remains of wharf, water reservoir, Buddhist vihara, Buddha pada, Buddha bronze image, brick structures and various types of pottery such as Rouletted ware which can be correlated with the descriptions given in the Sangam texts. Even the archaeological finds from the port sites of Arikamedu and Korkai match in many ways the description of the Sangam texts.

4. What are the objectives of maritime archaeology in India?

The objectives of maritime archaeology are as follows:

- To explore and excavate ports, shipwrecks and trade centres bringing to light the unknown past,
- To reconstruct the maritime history and interactions of India through maritime archaeological discoveries,
- To infer sea level and shoreline changes through coastal archaeological studies,
- To deploy geophysical equipment for locating submerged and buried artefacts and structures,
- To document and research traditional boatbuilding and navigational techniques,
- To disseminate the knowledge gained to scholars, researchers and students of similar disciplines, as well as to the general public.

5. What is the importance of maritime archaeological studies?

The results of exploration of ports, trade centres and shipwrecks help to reconstruct the maritime history, trade and cultural contacts of India with other countries in bygone ages. The rate of sea level and shoreline changes are inferred from coastal archaeological studies. The study and documentation of traditional boatbuilding and navigational techniques help us understand the skills gained by mariners in ancient times and show the types of boats and ships used in rivers, lakes and seas for various purposes. The outcome of research is disseminated among the scholars, researchers, students of similar disciplines and general public, either through research publications, lectures or by print and visual media.

6. How are maritime archaeological data and information collected before undertaking offshore surveys?

- Literary information is collected on ports, maritime trade, navigational and shipbuilding technology and shipwrecks from various libraries and archives in India and abroad.
- Onshore exploration artefacts from a site help as a pointer to undertake offshore exploration.
- Scholars and experts in relevant subjects are consulted to learn the potential of archaeological sites.
- Interaction and discussion are made with local fishermen, scholars and villagers regarding shipwrecks, maritime remains and traditions of the region which help to know the presence of archaeological artefacts.
- Geophysical surveys are conducted to get signatures of remains of maritime activities on the surface and subsurface of the seabed.

7. How is local knowledge useful for maritime archaeology?

Local information or knowledge is found to be most useful and informative not only in India but also abroad in maritime archaeological research. Shipwrecks have been located and explored in Sunchi Reef, St George's Reef and the Amee Shoals off Goa and Poompuhar in Tamil Nadu on the basis of information collected from fishermen and local divers in that region. Similarly, shipwrecks have been located in Australia and Thailand after obtaining information from sailors and fishermen. In Turkey sponge divers provided information on shipwrecks that were subsequently explored and excavated. Artefacts have been collected off Portugal based on information from local divers. Other European countries have used available local knowledge and information to locate shipwrecks and submerged sites.

8. What are the methodologies adopted in maritime archaeological studies?

After obtaining information either from onshore findings, literary sources, or local fishermen and scholars, and based on the importance of the finds or period of a site, offshore exploration is planned and subsequently carried out. Prior to offshore exploration all official formalities, such as obtaining permission from concerned authorities (Customs, Police, Navy, Coast Guard and local administration), are made. A suitable size of boat for underwater exploration and divers is hired, if required. Survey techniques are decided upon and choice of equipment is made according to the nature of the site. Importantly, seasonal and sea conditions must be taken into account.

9. How are the team organized and how many professionals are involved in the whole process of exploring a site?

Generally, the team consists of team leader, dive master, diver archaeologists, photographer, surveyor, draughtsman, technicians to look after equipment and electronic gadgets, and a number of divers for assistance. If the number of divers is large it helps in various ways: more dives can be made, larger area can be covered, more output can be expected, deeper explorations can be carried out and diving work is not hampered. If funds are limited, of it the site is small or the duration of the project is short, then the requirement for personnel can be adjusted. It is always useful to have a large number of diver archaeologists in the team. If the project is in a remote area, it is useful to have a physician in the team.

10. How are the underwater explorations planned and executed?

It is essential to plan a detailed programme before undertaking underwater explorations so that the goals can be achieved. There should be detailed discussion among the members of the team on the plans, procedures and techniques, and all participants should be familiar with the techniques which will be adopted. It is imperative that everyone should have background knowledge and expertise on the subject. After completion of the first stage of the work the second stage of action should be ready for implementation. The plan will be different from site to site depending upon the site and its conditions, such as visibility.

11. How are research designs planned?

Research design is a plan of action for fulfilling the objectives of the project. Though there are no watertight compartments, some normal procedures can be followed, such as why the project should be undertaken, what could be its outcome, a strategy for fieldwork, a timetable for completion, availability of technology and techniques to be adopted, underwater excavation and documentation, recovery of artefacts and other finds, if any, and their conservation. Post fieldwork measures, including publication, all should be included in the research plan. The research design should be planned in such a manner that there should not be any difficulties while undertaking the project. Whatever problems are anticipated should be taken care of beforehand.

12. Is maritime archaeology a season bound study in India?

Yes, in India maritime archaeology is a season bound study. India is dependent on monsoons and during monsoon seasons underwater exploration is not possible because of rough seas and turbidity of water. Further, all the rivers of India discharge quantities of sediment into the sea and the water becomes turbid, the sea remains rough and visibility reduces to zero from the month of June to the end of September. During the off season research and analysis is carried out in the laboratory, or data is collected from various libraries and archives on other proposed sites. It is always preferable to undertake onshore exploration after monsoons and offshore explorations during fair weather and calm sea conditions.

CHAPTER FOUR

DIVING

1. What is diving?

In simple terms diving means plunging into water to undertake the assigned task. No references are available in recorded history of the earliest date of diving, but the evolution of the development of diving has been recorded. The early divers were able to spend limited duration in under water on a single breath. They could have remained under water for two to three minutes at a stretch. There are various forms of diving, which are classified as skin diving (free diving), breath held diving, bell diving, surface supply diving (commercial diving) and scuba diving.

2. What is the history of diving?

History gives no background information about when the first diving began and who were the first divers. Diving in the ocean is a very old practice. In earlier days diving was carried out in search of food and treasure. Most of this diving was done without any special equipment. The Greek historian, Herodotus mentioned that in 400 BC divers were used for military purposes. In later period the knowledge of diving was applied for scientific research, military operations and recreational purposes. In earlier times diving equipment consisted of a breathing tube to the diver's mouth, the upper end of the tube being supported on the surface by a float. Until the Middle Ages there were not many developments in diving systems. Closed diving dress and helmet were invented by Augustus Siebe in Germany in 1837. This was the greatest single advance made in the development of diving equipment; even today this dress is essentially unchanged throughout the world.

3. What is skin or free diving?

A skin diver dives by holding the breath in shallow water without using any type of diving apparatus or gear (Fig. 5). The duration of each dive depends on the ability of the individual to hold his or her breath as long as possible. Among all kinds of dive, skin or free diving is the earliest and oldest one and was carried out in search of treasure, sponges and pearls. Even today this practice still prevails in some parts of India and abroad.

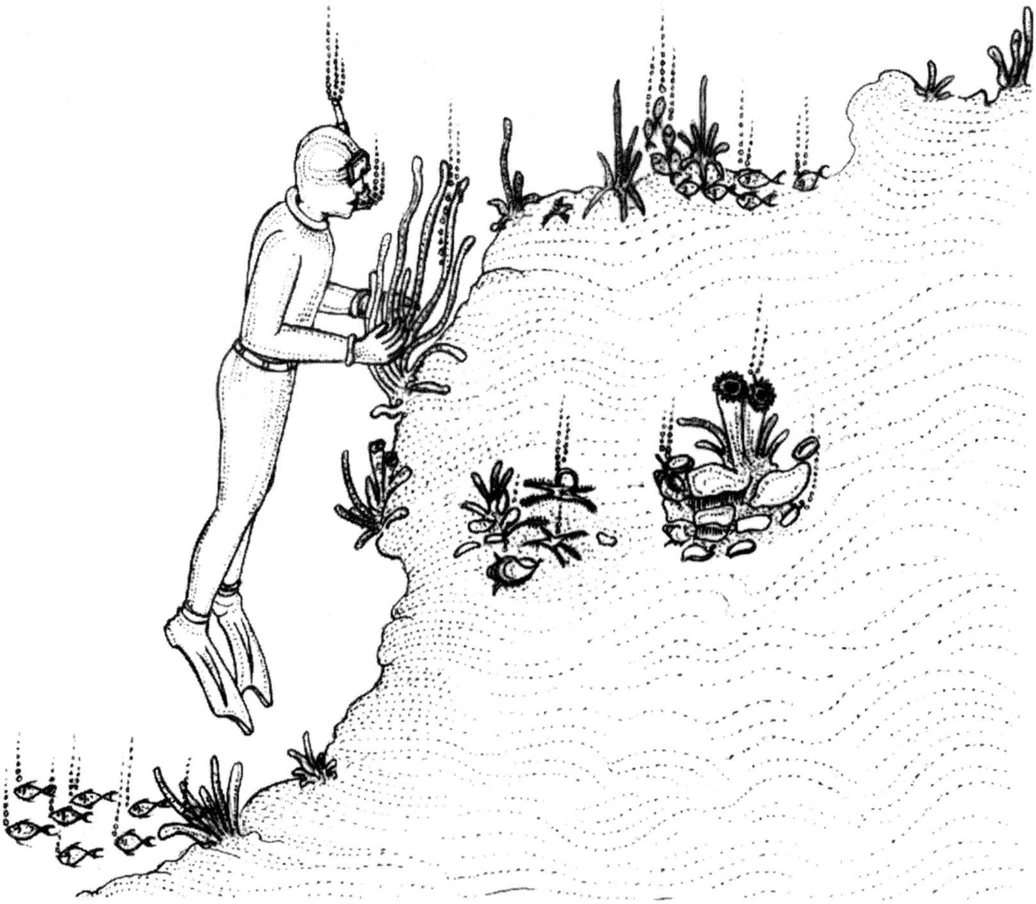

Fig. 5 Free diving

4. What is bell diving?

The diving bell is an early apparatus consisting of a hollow vessel or chamber, originally bell shaped, open at the bottom and supplied with air by a tube from above, by which one may descend into and work under water. During the time of Alexander the Great (330 BC), divers dived into the River Indus by diving bell to retrieve the bell from his ship. In the 16th century the true diving bell (Colimpha) was developed allowing a diver to work for an hour in Italy's Lake Nemi, near Rome, to locate Caligula's barges. This is the earliest reliable record of a diving bell in actual use. In the 17th century divers worked in very large diving bells. In the 1690s the idea was improved by Edmond Halley, English astronomer, and in the 18th century it was further developed by the Swede, Marten Triewalds.

5. What is surface supplied diving gear?

Surface supplied diving was developed by Andrew Becker in 1715. The equipment used for this kind of diving is known as Surface Demand Diving Equipment (SDDE). Prior to the invention of scuba diving gear, SDDE gear was used for all kinds of diving. This system enables divers to perform different kinds of underwater tasks and to remain in shallow waters for a longer period. For search in low visibility and for spot work this system really has no substitute. The system provides a direct link between divers and the surface; communication takes place through signals. Should divers be moved away by the current they can easily be brought onboard. Today commercial diving companies and some archaeologists use this system for undertaking various kinds of underwater tasks.

6. What kind of equipment makes a surface supplied diving gear?

Surface supplied diving system includes a low pressure (LP) air compressor and an air tank to store the compressed air. Attached to the tank are filters to purify the air, and demand valves to control the flow of air. An air hose of required length runs from the tank to the diver to supply breathing air (Fig. 6). The

Fig. 6 Surface supplied diving system

other requirements are mask, fins, weight belt, hand gloves, underwater compass and diver's knife.

7. Who invented scuba diving?

The first self-contained dive system was developed by William James in 1825. In a later period the whole scenario of diving changed with the invention of the 'aqualung' breathing system of diving gear by French Navy Commandant, Jacques Yves Cousteau and engineer Emile Gagnan in 1942 at Badol on the French Riviera. The invention of the aqualung has indeed revolutionised not only diving but also our understanding of the sea itself, enabling divers to explore the shallow edge of continental shelves to depths of 60 to 75 m. The scuba system helped in providing greater freedom to the divers' underwater movement and enriched the sport of diving all over the world. Throughout the world exploration of shipwrecks and submerged sites are mostly carried out by scuba systems.

8. What is scuba diving?

SCUBA (Self Contained Underwater Breathing Apparatus) diving gear consists of a portable tank carried on the back by shoulder straps, to store compressed air, a regulator to supply air from the tank to the diver at comfortable pressure. Before each dive a pressure gauge should be use on the tank to indicate the amount and pressure of the air inside. Instead of shoulder straps, a buoyancy compensator device (BCD) may be worn to allow the diver to adjust his or her buoyancy and to hold the tank on the diver's back. This system enables the diver to dive freely without any hindrance (Fig. 7). Scuba

Fig. 7 Diver with scuba gear

is simple, yet remarkable, in that it delivers air on demand at a pressure slightly above the ambient pressure. The scuba system is highly useful for underwater surveys, especially while operating an underwater scooter or underwater TV and still cameras, drawing, or using a communication system or hand held metal detector.

9. What kind of equipment comprises scuba diving gear?

Diving gear must be comfortable for underwater work. Too much equipment would lead to discomfort. Scuba diving gear consists of mask (for vision), snorkel (surface breathing), fins (for paddling or propulsion), a BCD (inflatable bladder) to aid in ascending and descending, air tank(s), valves, gauges to indicate water depth and amount of air in tank(s), dive skins (good protection from sun but not for thermal protection), wet suit (that allows entry of only a minimum quantity of water and provides reasonable comfort at moderate temperature), underwater watch (to know the duration of dive), underwater compass (to determine direction), knives (dive knives are used as tools), hood (protects head from cold water), gloves (protection of hands) and weight belt (to offset the buoyancy of the diver's body) (Fig. 8).

Fig. 8 Scuba diving gear

10. What is thermal protection and how divers protect themselves?

Thermal protection is determined by the water temperature, nature of work and physiology of the diver. But it is essential for divers to pay attention for their comfort at every stage of work underwater. For thermal protection different kinds of dive suits are worn by the divers. Dive skins are worn by the diver to protect from sun, coral cuts, scrapes, etc. For warm waters wet suits are preferred. Wet suits are made of neoprene, a synthetic material with a number of tint closed cells that are filled with nitrogen gas. Diver feels reasonable comfort at moderate temperature. Dry suits are most effective for passive thermal protection. Dry suits are designed from one piece suit with a waterproof zipper never allows water to enter inside and seals the wrist and neck. Dry suits are made from a variety of materials. In dry suit it is possible to dive in a variety of water temperature. The other variety is hot water suit; in this system hot water hose delivers heated water from the topside unit to the diver.

11. What is buoyancy in diving?

The buoyancy provided by water means divers experience weightlessness when they are submerged, in the same way that an astronaut experiences zero gravity. An object floats from positive buoyancy and sinks from negative buoyancy; if an object neither sinks nor floats it is neutrally buoyancy. The amount of buoyancy rendered by a liquid relies on the weight of the liquid. To control their position in the water column, divers wear a lead belt which makes them sink and a buoyancy compensator which, like a life-preserver, is worn around the shoulder to help them float. Any diver or object will be less buoyant in fresh water and more buoyant in salt water.

12. What is buddy diving and buddy line?

Buddy diving means a pair of divers operating as a unit, each responsible for the safety of the other. It is important for safe diving that divers are formed into buddy pairs. Generally new divers should be paired up with a minimum of one experienced diver. More than two divers can dive at a time but single diver is never allowed for safety reasons.

Generally, a buddy line is required in poor visibility conditions. A suitable length of rope 3 to 5 m long is ideal for a buddy line. The ends of the line are tied at suitable places to the divers in a way that leaves both hands of each diver free and does not their restrict movement.

13. What is shipwreck diving?

Shipwreck diving is one of the most popular forms of diving. It requires extra safety precautions if divers venture inside the wreck. Metal wrecks which are in a state of decay with loose objects or steel plates are a real hazard for divers. Similarly, while diving on a wooden hulled wreck never remove or pull any artefacts which are lying over it as these might be fragile, hence extra precautions are required. Never venture deep inside a wreck without ensuring the route. It is safest to use a line to mark the return route. Avoid excessive finning inside a wreck as it reduces visibility and sediment may be stirred up which takes a long time to settle down. Always carry an adequate reserve air tank and never run down your air supply. Never try to lift heavy object(s) from wrecks using BCD.

14. What are the institutes and organisations that offer diving courses in India and abroad?

In India, except for the Naval School of the Indian Navy, Cochin, Kerala no other governmental organisations offer diving courses. Details can be obtained from the Indian Navy, Cochin. In India, there are only a few private diving companies that offer scuba diving courses on payment but they do not teach maritime archaeology. The Nautical Archaeology Society (NAS), UK, is the premier society that offers certificate courses both on diving and maritime archaeology. Some times the society conducts courses in different parts of the world in association with institutes and organisations related to this discipline. NAS had organised the Part-I course, 'An Introduction to Underwater Archaeology' at NIO in 1990. The recreational scuba training programmes conduct courses on diving, shipwrecks and underwater archaeology. In the United States training for recreational diving is provided by the National Association of Underwater Instructors (NAUI): www.naui.com, and the Professional Association of Diving Instructors (PADI): *www.padi.com*; in the UK it is the British Sub Aqua Club: www.ukdiving.co.uk.

15. What are the factors which affect diving?

A number of environmental factors, including temperature, visibility, currents, bottom composition, sea animals and plant life, affect diving conditions. The temperature of water plays a major role in diving. Temperature changes as water depth increases and this may lead to loss of body heat. Diving in cold water requires special attention and special types of diving suits must be used.

Both surface and underwater currents are generated by wind, wave and seabed formation. Diving against the current and working in one causes exhaustion or fatigue. It is preferable to begin the dive against the current which will help while returning and it is also easier to move with the current. It is not advisable to struggle in strong current which leads to quick exhaustion.

Underwater visibility depends upon sea bottom composition. Sometimes visibility is reduced due to weather conditions, marine plankton or algae, movement of suspended material and muddy or turbid water. With restricted visibility it becomes difficult to undertake underwater tasks. Unless it is essential, avoid diving in poor visibility.

The types of seabed may include silt, clay, mud, rocks and corals. Avoid excessive finning and standing if seabed is silt, clay or mud. Chances of cuts and scratches may occur while diving in rocky and coral areas. Under such circumstances divers have to take more precautions.

Most underwater animals are timid or flee at the presence of diver(s). However, some aquatic animals and plants are potentially hazardous to divers. It is always better to avoid them. If you encounter a shark or barracuda unexpectedly remain calm at the seabed and when they go away, pass or move away from the area and try to return onboard.

16. Do sharks attack diver(s) suddenly?

Maximum care should be taken while diving in shark infested areas and it is always advisable to have cages or a Gemini (rubber inflatable boat) very close to the divers. Divers can even carry a push rod (a rubber tipped aluminium rod) with them. If a shark comes close then it can be pushed back with the push rod. Generally sharks never attack divers suddenly unless they are hungry for days or if they come to shallow waters for some reason. A shark gives two or three brushes to the diver with his body before attacking; the shark does this when it feels the diver is suitable for diet. Sharks never like intruders in their waters; when they see an intruder they put their side fins down and proceed towards diver. At that moment the diver should retreat from the area. There is no record that any maritime archaeologists have died from shark attack.

17. What diving safety measures should be followed?

In diving, safety precautions are most important. The diving master or the diving supervisor should ensure that all the diving equipment is free of problems and each component of diving gear is checked before the diver goes into the water. The diving team must be fit for diving and no one should have any sickness or medical problems. If someone is not well, he or she should not insist upon diving, especially in case of cold or sickness. Medical fitness is essential because general practitioners are unaware of diving sickness problems which may be dangerous to life. A particular standard system of diving principles should be followed. The team should be careful in situations where deep diving is planned and the diving log should be maintained properly.

CHAPTER FIVE

TOOLS FOR MARITIME ARCHAEOLOGICAL RESEARCH

1. What are the search methods adopted for maritime archaeology researches?

The main objectives of search methods in maritime archaeology are to demarcate exact locations of sites in the seabed. Basically, two different methods are adopted for locating the site(s). One is geophysical survey and the other is physical searches by divers. In geophysical survey equipment is deployed for locating and identifying site(s), whereas in physical searches diver archaeologists carry out exploration on the seabed to locate the submerged remains. The geophysical survey is more free of risk than diving.

2. What is the geophysical equipment deployed for maritime archaeological researches?

Geophysical equipment such as echosounder, side-scan sonar, magnetometer, sub-bottom profiler, sparkers, etc., are generally deployed for maritime archaeological explorations. This equipment is deployed depending on the suitability and objectives of the project. State-of-art models with portable sizes, high resolutions, digital manipulation, video output and integrated with other equipment are available. These are definitely better than models of older design. An extensive area has been explored in Dwarka, Poompuhar and

Mahabalipuram waters by deploying geophysical equipment such as echosounder, side-scan sonar, magnetometer, sub-bottom profiler and sparkers. In the course of geophysical survey shipwrecks, submerged channels and outcrops of rocks are noticed.

3. What is echosounder?

The echosounder unit consists of a transmitter, a receiver and a transducer. The system provides valuable information in identifying submerged objects lying on the seabed (Fig. 9). A suitable combination of power and frequency of the signals improves resolution of the object(s), which helps in its identification(s). High power provides better penetration of signal whereas higher frequency of signal gives better resolution and clarity. The echosounder is used to learn and record the nature of the bathymetry or topography of the sea floor and also the water depth of a particular area or survey area.

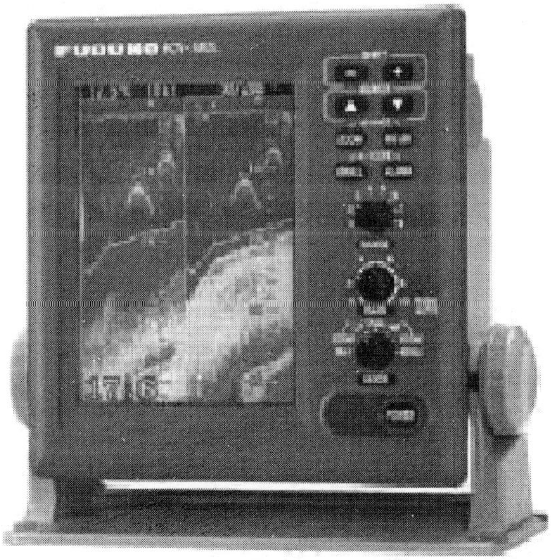

Fig. 9 Echosounder

4. How does the echosounder work?

Echosounder works on the principle of echo and short sound pulse frequencies, which are generated and transmitted vertically towards the sea floor. These sound pulses travel through the water column, hit the seabed, and then return and reflect on the echogram. These echoes on reaching the transducer are collected and the time required for the sound to travel both ways is measured and the water depth is calculated. The reflected sound pulses are collected by the same transducer and converted into electrical signals fed to the receiver and then to the recorder.

It is well known that the seabed is not always even and flat and the presence of shoals, coral reefs, ridges, banks, sea mounts and shipwrecks in the near shore zone are hazardous for navigation. When the echosounder passes over an object on the sea floor, it displays a pinnacle on the echogram. It is possible to interpret archaeological or non-archaeological objects based on echograms.

5. What is a side-scan sonar?

Sonar stands for Sound Navigation and Ranging. The side-scan sonar is a tool used for scanning the lateral topography on the seabed to detect shipwrecks and other artefacts of archaeological interest which may lie there. The side-scan sonar system includes a tow fish, towing cable and graphic recorder (Fig. 10). Beeps are sent from, and received by, a fish that is pulled behind the search ship. The signals are sent in a wide angular pattern down to the bottom. The images which are recorded on the graphic recorder resemble aerial photographs. Subsequently these images are collected and interpreted.

Fig. 10 Side-scan sonar, cable and towing fish

6. How does the side-scan sonar work?

Sonar works on exactly the same principle as the echosounder. The tow fish of the sonar is towed behind a vessel. While being towed it sends out sound waves in two separate fan shaped beams. These pulses of energy are reflected back to either side of the tow fish and then recorded on a rotating drum. The received signals are interpreted and displayed graphically. The return time of the pulses depends upon the distance. As the fish advances, an image is displayed on a monitor or a paper plotter which shows man-made or natural objects that protrude above the seabed, although not with photographic resolution. This system is widely used to locate shipwrecks, archaeological artefacts and submerged features. In the recent past a lot of development has been made in higher resolution of side-scan sonar images.

7. What is multibeam sonar and how does it work?

Multibeam sonar is a recent development used for surveying the seabed. This system is permanently attached to the centre portion of the hull of the vessel and not towed like side-scan sonar. It is widely used for hydrographic survey. It provides fan shaped coverage of the sea floor. Multibeam sonar measures and records the time for the acoustic signal to travel from transducer to seabed and back to the receiver. With this system it is possible to generate a three dimensional image of the seabed and with a special type of software the data can be analysed to know the seabed features, depth and images of the objects or artefacts lying on the seabed, including shipwrecks. During its recent use in the Persian Gulf a steel hulled shipwreck was located.

8. What is magnetometer?

Magnetometer is an electronic device that has immense value for marine archaeological research. It is an important underwater equipment used to detect buried or submerged ferromagnetic materials on or in the sea floor. A number of magnetometer surveys have been conducted both in Indian and foreign waters for locating shipwrecks in particular. The proton magnetometer is very precise and effective in locating shipwrecks. Shipwreck sites containing iron in the form of hull fastening and fittings, ballast, cannon, shot and iron anchors can set up magnetic anomalies. The proton magnetometer was introduced in underwater archaeological surveys for locating shipwrecks by Prof. E. T. Hall of the Research Laboratory for Archaeology at Oxford.

9. How does the magnetometer work?

Magnetometers measure the strength of the earth's magnetic field and can detect variations in this field caused by the presence of ferrous material or objects. The magnetometer is towed behind the survey vessel. The sensor or detector had should be lowered to the required depth so that the magnetometer can cover a large area and its output can be satisfactory. The magnitude of the field induced in an object depends on the size, shape, orientation and magnetic susceptibility of the object. Further, the magnitude of the anomaly depends on the depth of burial of the object, and the distance and orientation of the magnetometer. Thus, during deployment of the magnetometer, the size and range of the object can be roughly estimated. The direction and intensity of the earth's field also influences the magnitude of the induced field.

10. What are the recent developments in the use of geophysical equipment in maritime archaeological studies?

Recently, the Western Australia Maritime Museum (WAMM) used a combination of magnetometer and side-scan sonar for a successful survey. The magnetometer was located reasonably close to the side scan tow fish; it passed the information about the seabed and the distance of the detector head from the bottom. All these data were then combined within the side scan computer data logger. If the magnetometer tow fish is deployed a short distance behind the side-scan sonar, the side scan trace can be used to determine the height of the unit above the seabed, so that when a magnetic anomaly is encountered its mass can be estimated from the approximate equation. In this manner it is possible to log the information on the magnetic field strength; as the information is geo-referenced it creates magnetic contour plans. To get high resolution data and information it is best to undertake the survey first and investigate the anomalies afterwards. Once the survey is completed the data can be plotted either manually or computer generated.

11. What is the sub-bottom profiler?

The sub-bottom profiler is an acoustic tool used for detecting shipwrecks and other archaeological artefacts buried below the surface of the seabed. It includes a tow fish, a towing cable and a graphic recorder. It works on the same principle as echosounder but with a lower operating frequency allowing penetration through sand and silt. With a sub-bottom profiler one can obtain a profile of the sea floor or the layers of sediment and rock below the sea floor.

12. How does the sub-bottom profiler work?

A sub-bottom profiler is a bottom penetrating vertical sonar system. The sub-bottom profiler detects artefacts which are either buried partially or fully in the seabed. The working principle of a sub-bottom profiler is similar to the echosounder, but seismic profiling uses a stronger energy source from the surface and then measures the strength of the reflected energy. In this system the sound pulse is transmitted directly at the seabed in a conical shape. The return echoes below the seabed as well as from the seabed are electronically processed and continuously recorded on a graphic display to create an image called the sub-bottom profile. The profiler gives online recording features of the bottom and sub-bottom of the sea floor, which enable marine geoscientists and archaeologists to distinguish features of geological or archaeological interest.

13. What is a boomer and sparker system?

Submerged objects buried deeply in compact sediment which cannot be identified or delineated by the sub-bottom profiler can be detected by boomer and sparker. The boomer and sparker which generate high power signals can induce deeper penetration of the sediments and enable scientists to identify the deeply buried objects. In this system the power selection of the signals has to be maintained properly. If not, the high power may give a ghost image and low power gives weak signals. On the other hand low power gives weak incoming signals and may deny useful and valuable evidence. The K Joule power has been found suitable for 40 to 100 m water depth and good results have been obtained by using this power. Depending upon the sedimentary formations where palaeo-channels were buried this system can be used.

14. What is a metal detector and how does it work?

Metal detectors are an inexpensive and effective remote sensing device, although Hi-tech and expensive models tend to have better functions, displays and sensitivity to certain type of metal and metallic artefacts. Metal detectors can be deployed to identify metallic remains in archaeological sites even when no surface evidence exists. Underwater metal detectors are different from surface metal detectors and are an important tool for underwater archaeological research. Nowadays the metal detectors are pulse-induced. Currently, metal detectors are able to detect ferrous and non-ferrous metals. There are two types of metal detectors: Hand held (Fig. 11) and vessel (boat) towed (Fig. 12). Hand held metal detector surveys should be conducted systematically, either after setting a grid

Fig. 11 Hand held metal detector

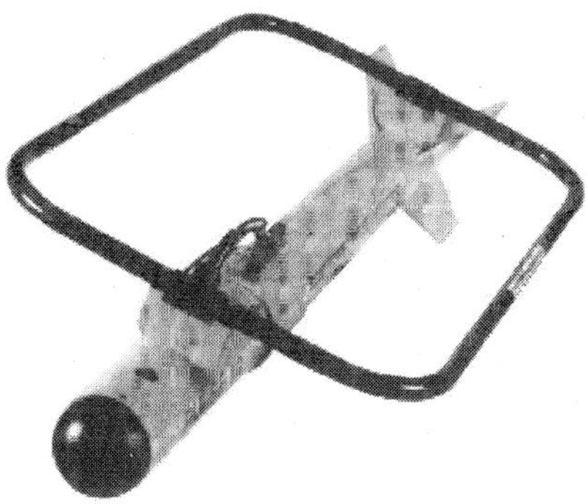

Fig. 12 Boat towing metal detector

by jackstay or a circular search pattern, whereas a boat towed metal detector is used like side-scan sonar. The metal detector reacts to the electrical conductivity of objects. The search coil contains a flat, circular coil of wire (antenna) that generates an electromagnetic field. When the search coil of the metal detector runs over or comes in close contact with metallic objects an electrical eddy current is produced and detected by the unit. It can be seen in the meter placed on the unit and a beep sound is heard through the earphone.

15. What is the differences between hand held and boat towed metal detectors?

Pulse 8x is the hand held metal detector which is carried by archaeologists to search for buried metal objects in the seabed. It has the capacity to detect any kind of metal within a range of 1.5 to 2m. This can be used up to a depth of 50 m. It is a watertight sealed chamber housing a coil powered by a rechargeable 14 volt battery. The charged battery runs for four hours at a stretch. A hand held metal detector is very handy and very useful in shallow water surveys.

Pulse 12x, on the other hand, is a boat towed metal detector consisting of a 0.6 m by 0.90 m coil, a towable fish, a pre-amp, a 100 m cable and a control box. For underwater use, the coil is mounted on the fish and is towed at any depth down to 100 m. The fish sails through the water at a depth determined by the speed of a boat and tows the coil very flat and directly below the boat. Pulse detectors operate by transmitting a stream of high energy magnetic pulses (one hundred per second), from the coil. After each pulse is transmitted, the unit then 'listens', using the coil as the receiving antenna. When a transmitted pulse hits a metal object, a magnetic field is induced in the object. This causes eddy currents to flow in the metal, which in turn generates a second magnetic field. This field is picked up by the coil, amplified and then displayed by the meter and heard in the speaker. For exploring a large area a boat towed metal detector is found highly efficient. Both hand held and boat towed metal detectors are used extensively in Goa and Poompuhar waters.

16. What are the visual survey equipments used for underwater exploration?

Geophysical equipment such as remote sensing tools gives signatures of the presence of artefacts which cannot be seen, whereas visual survey tools help to show remains lying above the seabed. The visual survey tools used for underwater explorations are: Underwater Scooter, Remotely Operated Vehicle (ROV),

Autonomous Underwater Vehicles (AUV) and Human-Occupied vehicles (HOV) or Submersibles. Visual survey equipment helps in identifying objects whether they are manmade or natural. Nowadays this equipment is used extensively for underwater exploration and inspection both in shallow and deeper waters.

17. What is an underwater scooter?

An underwater scooter is also known as a diver propulsion vehicle (DPV), a battery propelled, neutrally buoyant, watertight, cylindrical vehicle. Two types of underwater scooters are available in the market. A diver wearing scuba gear rides or is towed by the scooter and can explore at a desired depth without fatigue or much effort for a maximum duration. This enables a larger area to be explored in less time then by swimming (Fig. 13). Compass and depth gauges are fitted on the scooter so that the diver can see the direction and water depth while undertaking operations. The underwater speed can be controlled according to the requirement. There are certain restrictions on underwater scooters in terms of depth and duration, but they have been widely used in underwater exploration off Dwarka and Poompuhar. It is advisable to charge the battery after every use.

Fig. 13 Underwater scooter

18. What is a remotely operated vehicle (ROV)?

Fig. 14 Remotely operated vehicle (ROV)

An ROV is essentially a watertight housing system fitted with a video camera which can take underwater pictures and transmit them back to the ship or boat via a cable connection (Fig. 14). The ROV can be manoeuvred in any direction with its propellers, which are controlled by a joystick on the surface vessel that has deployed it. If the seabed is uneven and rocky, or shoals are present, maximum care should be taken to prevent the ROV from striking rocks. The use of ROVs in deep water archaeological studies and site inspection is a new development. The ROV is considered as one of the best underwater tools to be deployed for pre-disturbance surveys of any site. The other advantage with ROV is that it can be used for long duration in deep water till the end of the firsthand survey. In the recent past several shipwrecks have been discovered in deep waters by deploying ROV. Among the important shipwrecks were the *Titanic*, the *Bismark* and the *HMS Hood*.

19. What is an autonomous underwater vehicle (AUV)?

Fig. 15 Autonomous underwater vehicle

An autonomous underwater vehicle (AUV) is an underwater robot which is not remote controlled but operates with artificial intelligence. AUVs are powered by rechargeable batteries (Fig. 15), but some larger AUVs are powered by aluminium-based semi fuel cells. Just like the ROV, the AUV is used instead of divers to undertake difficult tasks in deeper waters. Most deep water shipwrecks can only be investigated or explored with AUVs and submersibles, but AUVs can go very deep without needing the pressure hull of submarines used to protect humans. AUVs are increasingly used in foreign countries for offshore exploration, ocean science and defence purposes.

20. How is the AUV found suitable for maritime archaeological explorations?

After the invention of AUV intensive efforts have been made for its commercial use. Since it is equipped with a high resolution multi-beam echosounder, chirp side-scan sonar, sub-bottom profiler and conductivity temperature depth (CTD). The CTD profiler is regularly used by oceanographers to measure the salinity and temperature of the water mass with respect to depth. Further, an AUV can survey a large area ranging from shallow depth to deeper waters down to 3000 m and more. AUVs were used for the survey of offshore oil and gas pipeline off the Gulf of Mexico. In the course of the survey two shipwrecks were reported in 1500 m water depth: the *Robert E. Lee* and the *U-166*. The *Robert E. Lee*, an American passenger freighter bound from Trinidad to New Orleans, was steaming across the Gulf of Mexico with its naval escort, *PC 566*. It was struck by a single torpedo launched from the German submarine *U-166*, which had been patrolling in the area. The lost of *U-166* was mystery and its discovery 140 miles east of where it was thought to have been lost solved a long standing shipwreck mystery in the Gulf of Mexico. The detection of wrecks through AUV survey confirms its suitability for maritime archaeological exploration.

21. What is a submersible?

The ROV and AUV are autonomous and cost-effective tools. However, they do not solve the problem of deep water survey using the naked eye. Manned, or human-occupied submersibles provide a means for maritime archaeologists to access the seabed to locate valuable artefacts visually. The introduction of manned submersibles which were developed during the 1960s and 1970s is the latest underwater tool used for all kinds of visual underwater research throughout the world. The manned submersible consists of four major components: a pressure hull, propeller(s), buoyant material and observational instruments. The shallow water manned submersibles can go down to 300 ft (92 m) water depth or more and can carry two persons who can stay for six hours under water in 1 atmospheric pressure and are used for various underwater surveys, explorations and inspections such as: environmental assessment, archaeological explorations (Fig. 16), geological surveys, reef and fish monitoring, tourism development, benthic studies and shellfish resources. The INA Bodrum, Turkey has procured the shallow water SEAmobile 'Carolyn', a two-person submersible with which fourteen previously unknown ancient shipwrecks were discovered in just one month.

Fig. 16 Manned submersible

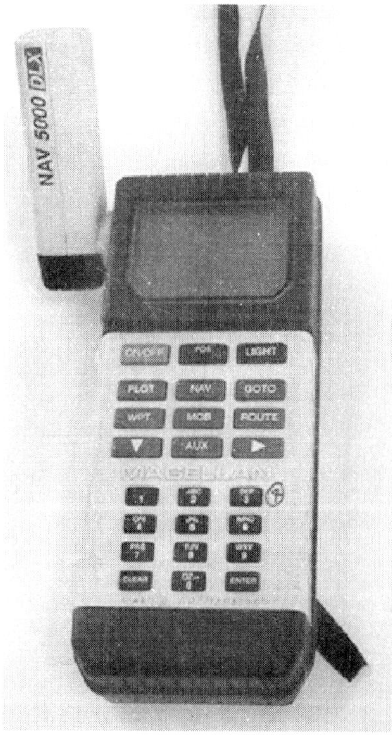

Fig. 17 Handheld GPS

22. What is the Global Positioning System?

The Global Positioning System (GPS) is a satellite based unit powered by pencil cells which helps navigation and allows determination of its exact position on the earth. GPS, introduced in 1988, is the most reliable and widely used system around the world. Four to five navigation satellites continuously send fix positions to every part of the earth round the clock. The receiver of the GPS calculates the user's position on the earth accurately. Accuracy, however, varies from system to system. Varieties of GPS systems are available in the market, but the Magellan model NAV 5000 DLX GPS is used for obtaining positions during maritime archaeological investigations in India (Fig. 17).

23. How does the GPS obtain its positions?

GPS collects data from satellites on five channels to compute position, elevation, velocity and navigation data. Once a satellite signal is received, it takes about 12 to 30 seconds to complete data on the location. The accuracy of the Magellan model NAV 5000 DLX GPS is 25 to 100 metres. One should keep this in mind while using the data. The other advantage of the GPS is that if the geo-coordinates of the site are already available then the coordinates are entered and guide the use to the location and give the distances. For obtaining an exact position regular readings should be taken for some time and the mean value computed. Nowadays to obtain a more accurate position of the working site DGPS is used.

24. What is a Differential Global Positioning System and how does it work?

In the Differential Global Positioning System (DGPS), a technique is used to improve positioning or navigational accuracy by determining the positioning error at a known location. In DGPS, two receivers work simultaneously, one is at the reference station and other is at a mobile one (either on boat or ship). The reference station generates corrections to all visible satellites and transmits them to mobile station by a radio link. The mobile receiver combines its own observed ranges from satellites. The corrections are received from reference stations, to arrive at a differentially corrected range, which is almost free from all errors common to both receivers. The accuracy of the mobile unit's position can be improved by 1 m, which otherwise would be around 5 to 15 metres. The DGPS system is most commonly used for its reliable surface positions while carrying out archaeological investigations.

25. What instruments were used prior to the invention of GPS?

Fig. 18 Sextant

Prior to the invention of GPS, the Sextant and Miniranger were used for obtaining the position of a work site. The sextant is a navigational instrument used for measuring solar and stellar heights. It has been used on land sites since the 16th century and its naval version was developed in 1757 by Captain John Campbell. The name refers to a sixth of a circumference -60°. Thus, the sextant can measure angles to 120°. It measures vertical, horizontal and diagonal angles.

The sextant was one of the most useful optical position fixing tools for coastal surveying. It is basically a protractor and telescope linked by mirrors which allow an angle between two separate features to be measured. From the boat the surveyor takes two angles between three selected features on the shore. The angles are transferred to a chart to fix the position of the site (Fig. 18).

26. How does the Miniranger work?

The Miniranger unit consisting of a range console with omni directional antenna is installed onboard. The base stations should be installed at known onshore fixed points. The electronic position fixing system works in 'C' band on a line-of-sight principle. When the system is in operation the mobile station transmits microwave signals at 5570 MHz. The base stations receive these signals and retransmit them at 5480 MHz; they are in turn received by the mobile station. The time elapsed is converted by the range console into distances that are displayed. From these two distances the position of the boat is calculated with respect to the land stations. During offshore survey the fix is taken at about one minute intervals and corresponding marks are recorded on the equipment for correlation. Based on ranges obtained from two stations an exploration site can be approached even when marker buoys are missing, and working sites can be reached.

27. What is underwater documentation and when is it carried out?

In simple terms the method of recording underwater features is known as underwater documentation. The documentation can be done either by underwater drawing or photography and videography. All these are equally important for recording and interpreting discoveries and are useful for publication. Before documentation it is essential to remove the overburden on the features so that they can be seen clearly. It is always preferable to document discoveries during good visibility and fair weather. While recording it is essential to place a scale near objects and drawing should be prepared on graph material for easy understanding. The length of the scale should not be longer than the size an object.

28. What are the tools deployed for underwater documentation?

Underwater videography is the latest addition for recording discoveries whereas drawing and photography are the traditional methods of documentation. In the recent past deep water findings have been documented through ROVs and submersibles. These systems provide visual information on both living and non-living (natural) features in the underwater world. However in shallow waters both photography and videography have their own places and importance, but for specific purposes one is usually better suited than the other. Photography is best for individual recording of artefacts, small objects or features and marine animals, whereas videography is best suited for particular situations or events. In photography and videography, the size, colour and condition of the artefact can be obtained, whereas in drawing the shape, elevation and section can be shown.

Fig. 19 Nikon underwater camera

29. How is underwater photography carried out?

Still photography provides an effective means of recording underwater archaeological finds and site remains. However, obtaining a clear image and proper recording is critical. Whenever artefacts are photographed a scale must be placed near them to help determine the exact sizes of the artefacts.

In recent times the most promising camera used for underwater photography is the Nikon (Fig. 19) with a lens of 35 mm focal length. A wide angle lens allows the photographer to come closer to the subject. A Nikon camera with a 15-20 mm wide angle lens is ideal for archaeological documentation. Electronic or bulb flashguns are available for Nikons. Colour or black and white films are used for the purpose. Today cameras are available having the facility to record live and still digital images. They have been found to be suitable for recording underwater discoveries.

30. What is a colour watch and underwater video camera system?

The video recording system consists of an underwater camera, colour monitor, keyboard, DVC recorder and umbilical cable. The underwater discoveries can be seen onboard on the monitor, which is attached to a wide angle lens camera with an underwater light and umbilical cable. The system converts images captured underwater into digital form through a decoder and records on mini DVC (digital video cassette). The monitor has a light control, which can be illuminated underwater in three modes depending on requirement and seabed conditions. The system has audio record DVC and VHS output. The system facilitates recording of underwater communications between divers and a controller onboard (Fig. 20).

Fig. 20 Colour watch camera system

The camera unit is fitted with a water resistant chamber and can be deployed down to 100 m water depth. The diver takes only the camera attached to an underwater light. During good visibility the camera can cover an area of 2 to 3 m, but in poor visibility only up to 0.5 m. The required information such as date, depth, site name, name of the diver, location and other details can be typed using the keyboard writer and the same can be recorded on the DVC if required.

31. How is the Sony Handycam used for recording underwater findings?

Fig. 21 Sony Handycam camera and Sony housing

The normal movie Sony HI 8 or Sony DVC cameras can be fitted in the Sony housing which is a watertight chamber (Fig. 21) and deployed for recording of underwater discoveries. The advantage of this unit is that the diver can move freely anywhere under water to record archaeological artefacts and features, topography of the seabed, marine life and environment. While using this system it is always preferable to dive with scuba gear. This system can be deployed in water as deep as 40 m. The quality of recording depends upon the visibility and nature of the site. Although for additional light battery power halogen bulbs are mounted on the unit. This system has been used for recording underwater discoveries off the coast of Goa, Mahabalipuram and Saurashtra.

32. What is underwater drawing?

Fig. 22 Underwater drawing

Underwater drawing is another method of underwater documentation. The drawing is prepared on polyester tracing (Garware) film, which is fixed on a suitable sized aluminium drawing board with a graph sheet placed below the polyester tracing film (Fig. 22). Ordinary H or HB pencils are used for underwater writing. It is suggested that underwater drawing should be carried out during good visibility so that the object can be seen clearly from all angles and nothing is missed. The artefacts are drawn *in situ* along with proper measurement, bearing and description. Recording date, time, water depth, object, location and direction are noted on the drawing board, which help while finalising the drawings. The final drawings can be used for various kinds of publications.

33. How are underwater observations recorded?

Fig. 23 Diver recording underwater finds in slate

Maritime archaeologists carry with them a white acrylic board (25 x 18 cm) with a pencil attached. The findings and other features which are observed in course of exploration are written down on the board along with water depth, date and time. If necessary, sketches are also prepared. This information should be transferred to the log book or in the register while working or at the end of the day. This enables any error found to be checked again. These recorded observations are essential while finalising the report and reduce last moment confusion. Sometimes details are forgotten entirely, hence they should be noted down properly.

In addition to acrylic board, we also use an underwater slate made of a half portion of a PVC pipe. It is tied on the hand with Velcro (hook and loop fasteners) (Fig. 23). The merit of this slate is that it remains on the hand and writing on it is very easy under water; further it does not hinder the diver's movements.

CHAPTER SIX

EXPLORATION AND SEARCH TECHNIQUES

1. What is onshore exploration?

Exploration which is carried out between the land and the sea is known as onshore exploration. Onshore exploration is carried out to study archaeological remains of habitations, ports, trade centres and shipwrecks. Discoveries include pottery, coins, seals, sealing, beads, cargo remains, both stone and brick structures, sculptures and other antiquities, which provide clues to history, and to their importance, contacts and purposes. Onshore exploration helps to determine the importance of a site and prompt underwater exploration. Sometimes onshore exploration is confined to the intertidal zone.

2. What is offshore exploration?

Exploration which is carried out in the sea to locate the material remains of human activities is known as offshore exploration. Offshore exploration is undertaken either after ascertaining the onshore background, on the basis of descriptions given in literature or locations marked on Hydrographic charts, marine records or information collected from local scholars, divers and fishermen. Before undertaking offshore exploration all necessary formalities and requirements are taken into account and sea conditions of the working area is also considered. It has been observed that input provided by fishermen and divers has been found most valuable in undertaking offshore exploration.

3. How is offshore exploration carried out?

Offshore exploration is carried out either by deploying geophysical equipment or visual searches by archaeologists, volunteers and hired divers. Geophysical surveys provide information on the nature of the seabed and objects lying on or buried in the seabed which cannot be seen; they may show anomalies whereas visual equipment provides more certain indications of the presence of archaeological remains. Hence underwater searches by maritime archaeologists become imperative. Visual searches are carried out either by archaeologists or by deploying electronic instruments such as underwater scooter, ROVs, and manned submersibles. Regardless of the equipment used, it is often essential that archaeologists should actually dive during maritime archaeological exploration or if volunteer/hired divers are engaged, archaeologists should be their buddy divers and help them to identify what they find.

4. What visual search techniques are followed in underwater searches?

Various types of underwater visual searches are undertaken by maritime archaeologists but these techniques are limited to a certain depth. Such techniques are chosen based on the objectives of the exploration, underwater visibility, sea conditions, and currents. These techniques, such as circular, swim line, jackstay and towing search are chosen to meet the objectives of the search. Each type of search technique has its own importance and merits. Such techniques have been followed during underwater exploration in India both for maritime archaeological and other oceanographic studies.

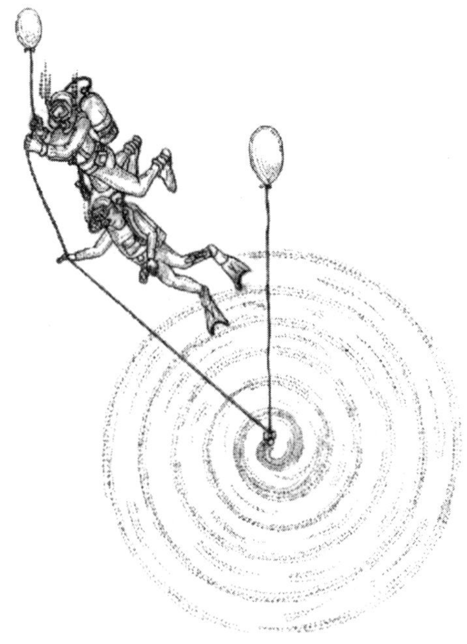

Fig. 24 Circular search pattern

5. What is a circular search pattern?

A circular search is one of the simplest and most effective methods in underwater archaeological survey. Divers using this method need a required length of rope or cable. One end of the rope is tied to a known point or held by a diver and the other diver will take rounds around the first diver by varying the radius. Once the diver completes a full round, some more cable will be released then another round will start. In this manner the diver will take bigger circles around the known point or the diver holding one end of the rope (Fig. 24). In the course of this search care should be taken about the overlapping of circles, fouling of rope and visual contacts between divers. If any archaeological objects are found those should be noted down and marked.

6. What is a swim line search pattern?

In a swim line search pattern two or more divers take a rope or make a line by maintaining a minimum distance between one another and undertake the search in a particular direction (Fig. 25). They should move at equal speed and should be able to keep in touch with each other constantly. While proceeding, divers should see the seabed clearly and record the findings and should not miss each other. To show the position of the divers and their movement any one diver can carry a marker buoy. Swim line searches are more effective in shallow waters. If current action prevails then divers should take more precautions; it is advisable to dive along with current because it may be difficult to dive against it.

Fig. 25 Swim line search pattern

7. What is a jackstay search pattern?

In this search pattern, first of all a jackstay line is laid on the seabed and marker buoys are tied at both the ends of the jackstay which will indicate its position and length. However, the length of the jackstay should not be too long or it may hinder the exploration. The length of the jackstay should depend upon the search area and nature of the site. Any kind of search will be fruitful if the visibility is good and seabed is even. Divers will start the search from the beginning of the jackstay to the end by following the swim line technique (Fig. 26). Once the search of jackstay area is completed, another area can be surveyed by repeating the same method. During poor visibility maximum care should be taken during jackstay search.

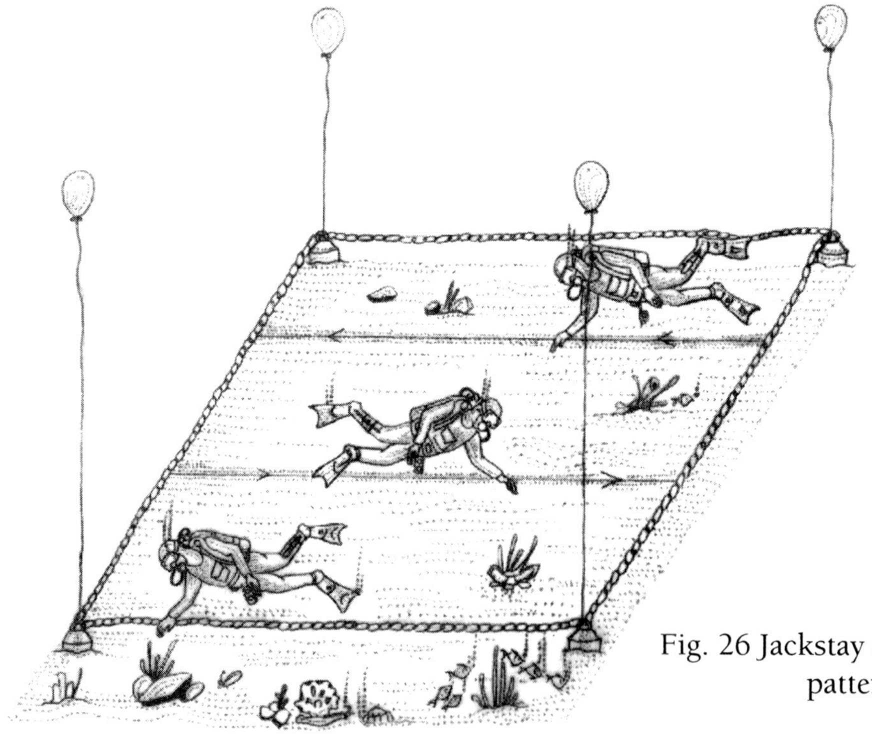

Fig. 26 Jackstay search pattern

8. What is towing search pattern?

Towing search is a common system of underwater survey. In it, two or more divers are towed behind a Gemini or a rubber boat by holding a rope or cable (Fig. 27). The length of the rope should be sufficient for the divers to control themselves while the boat is in motion. Surface communication with the divers is

Fig. 27 Towing search pattern

of benefit in this kind of survey. The speed of the boat should be such that the divers should not feel uncomfortable. To reduce the inherent risks to divers and pressure related illness a careful watch of the depth is important. Divers have to take maximum care in this search method because they are unaware of the topography and nature of the seabed, which may have sudden obstructions during a survey. The effectiveness of the towing search will depend on underwater visibility and the movement of the divers over the seabed. The positive point in this search is that a wide region can be covered in little time. The output of this type of survey depends on the onboard staff who controls the pattern of navigation.

9. What is a hand held metal detector survey?

Although metal detector survey is part of remote sensing, the hand held metal detector survey can be categorised under visual survey. In India the Pulse 8X hand held metal detector (JW Fishers) is being used for exploration. The hand held metal detector is a watertight chamber having the capacity to detect any kind of metal in a radius of 1.5 to 2 m and can be deployed as deep as 50 m. The range of the metal detector increases as the sizes of objects increase. Rechargeable batteries are used for operations which run for four hours at a stretch. Unlike magnetometers the hand held metal detector can detect both ferrous as well as non-ferrous metals and works on the pulse induction principle. The diver holds the metal detector and moves around on the seabed (Fig. 28). Wherever any metal anomalies are recorded the coil in the detector will amplify the signal and this will be displayed in the meter or by a beep which can be heard through the earphone.

Fig. 28 Underwater metal detector search and documentation

10. What is the pre-disturbance survey?

A preliminary survey is carried out to assess the nature of the seabed in and around the site without disturbing or lifting any of the archaeological objects or artefacts found. This technique is based upon use of known historical data in an unknown area. For this a detailed visual seabed survey is carried out by following any kind of search technique to determine the features of the seabed. During the course of pre-disturbance survey much attention is paid to natural features like rock outcrops, seabed topography, type of seabed, water depth, movement of sediments, current direction and nature of features. After the conclusion of a satisfactory pre-disturbance survey, decisions can be made for further surveys of a site.

11. How to undertake explorations in low and zero visibility?

Sometimes maritime archaeologists have to work in low and zero visibility where it is difficult to establish communication with buddy divers. Under such circumstances it is advisable to take the utmost care. Before diving there should be thorough discussion about the nature of the work and how to achieve the goal. This should be done on land before going under water. It should be decided who will do what and what should be the nature of movement under water and the duration of the dive. There should be pre-laid lines for the movement of divers from one place to another. Besides, presence of a standby diver is recommended and lifelines are useful. Having an underwater communication system on such occasions will be very fruitful for it increases the efficiency of work and the safety of the divers.

12. What is an underwater communication system and how does it work?

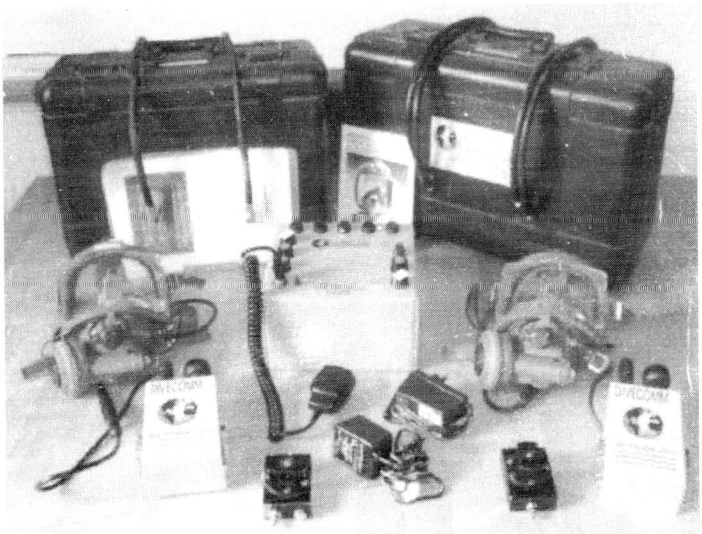

Fig. 29 Underwater communication system

Underwater communications carry the voice through signals in water. Various types of underwater communications systems are available, such as: acoustic telephones, wireless, sonic and ultrasonic. Their prime task is to send voice communications through water. The system consists of an electronic package carefully waterproofed, including battery, transducer (antenna), waterproof earphone(s), microphone and helmet or wide-vision face mask secured by belt buckles (Fig. 29). An underwater communication system is generally compact in design and completely self-contained. The divers will be wearing a helmet or wide-vision face mask connected with earphone and microphone. When the diver wants to talk, he simply presses the PTT button provided on the wide-vision mask.

13. What are earlier methods of underwater communication?

Before the invention of the underwater communication system traditional methods were followed to communicate from surface to divers. When a SDDE system of diving was the practice the communication was managed by rope, cable or diver's hose. There are 6 kinds of signals which are as follows: 1 signal = ok; 2 signals = lifting of cable or material; 3 signals = lowering of cable or material; 4 signals = come up or coming up; 4 signals + 2 bells = pull me up or come up immediately; 2 bells followed by one pull = found the object underwater or did you find? (A fast double pull is the bell whereas a normal pull is a signal). Even today this practice is followed in scuba and surface supply diving systems.

14. How were divers called to the surface?

If divers are undertaking an assigned task using the communication system it is trouble free to recall them to the surface. If divers are diving on SDDE system or were scuba divers who carried rope or cable they were called by giving signals. The other traditional method is to call the divers either by beating or hammering constantly on a metal object because sound passes under water. All these practices are followed in India.

CHAPTER SEVEN

UNDERWATER SURVEYS AND EXCAVATION

1. What is the direct survey method?

The direct survey method has been developed for underwater archaeology to record accurate seabed locations of finds. It is a form of three dimensional triangulation measuring directly three or more points of precisely known position. This means measuring the distance from each new point to three established datum points with a tape measure. The calculations can be done either manually or on a computer. Recently programmes have been developed to use four known points which can quantify the degree of accuracy of the data and location errors in measurements. Direct survey method is one of the best methods of underwater survey.

2. What is the triangulation survey method?

A triangulation survey is a simple form of survey done by measuring horizontally from two known points to a third and then producing a scale drawing using a compass to draw an arc from each point on the plan to the distance measured. Where the two arcs intersect gives the plotted position of the third point. Accuracy is increased if measurements are taken from three known points because survey or drawing errors then become immediately obvious. The triangulation survey method is used during underwater exploration and excavation in Indian waters.

3. How are the underwater excavations carried out?

Underwater excavations are not like land excavations and much depends on the nature of the seabed topography. Loose materials deposited on the seabed can be removed by hand fanning. Instead of digging into the seabed, as on land, overburden is often removed by means of transportation through two devices: airlift and water dredge. If the seabed is compact and hard, it is likely that underwater excavations can be carried out and stratigraphy can be observed. However, underwater excavation may not be possible if the seabed is rocky. In case of low or zero visibility either a cofferdam or steel enclosure can be erected around the site and water is pumped out of cofferdam to improve the visibility. This method was adopted for undertaking excavation of the Betsy in York River, York town, Virginia.

4. What is cofferdam and its uses in underwater excavations?

Cofferdam is a watertight enclosure from which water is pumped to expose the bed of a body of water in order to undertake the construction or other hydraulic work and in case of maritime archaeology to excavate an underwater site or a shipwreck. After installation of the cofferdam the water of the site is pumped out and the excavation work is carried out. This helps the diver to work freely without struggling in strong current and choppy waves. Cofferdams also improve visibility of the sites where visibility is low. By building cofferdams several shipwrecks have been excavated and the important ones were the French ship La Salle's *La Belle* in 1686 and the *Betsy* of 1772 at Yorktown, Virginia, USA. Recently, in Venice a 'Gondala' was excavated using cofferdam.

5. What is airlifting and how does it work?

Unlike land excavations, underwater excavations are carried out either by airlift or water dredge, which are used to remove sediment by suction. An airlift is an underwater excavation tool which has been used by archaeologists since 1950. It consists of a rigid, nearly vertically pipe, 10 to 15 cm in diameter. Air is introduced into the lower end of the pipe, usually from a hose running to a compressor on the surface. As this air passes upwards through the pipe it expands, creating suction that draws into the pipe water and other materials such as sediment and spoil. Sometimes archaeological artefacts are accidentally sucked up, but these can be rescued if the discharge from the top of the airlift pipe is collected. While operating the airlift, however, the diver holds the lower end of the pipe and takes care of small, fragile artefacts so that they are not damaged (Fig. 30). The efficiency of an airlift depends on its design, diameter of the tube, air pressure and volume, water depth, length of pipe, size and density of material being lifted, and height of discharge. Airlifting has been carried out in the Dwarka, Bet Dwarka, Goa, Somnath and Poompuhar waters of India.

6. What is a water dredge and how does it work?

The function of a water dredge is similar to an airlift, but it is operated more in a horizontal position than a vertical one. In a water dredge water is supplied from a pump instead of air from a compressor. Its mode of operation, however, is similar to that of an airlift, although it can be used in shallow water than an airlift. Another advantage is that the spoil removed from the site by a horizontal dredge can be discharged on the seabed itself, maintaining good underwater visibility at the site. Further, advantages over an airlift are ease to use, requirement of less space onboard, and greater adjustability. In India, airlifting has been used extensively but not the water dredge.

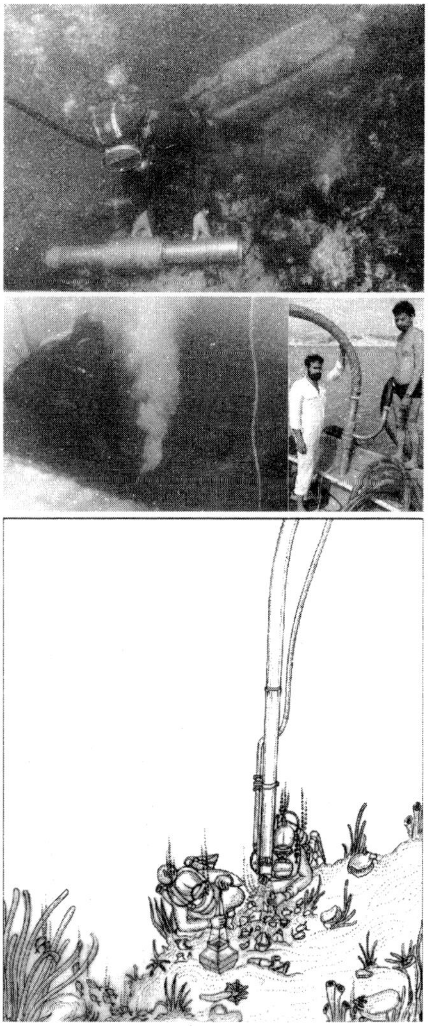

Fig. 30 Airlifting operation

7. How are the positions of discoveries fixed?

During exploration if any archaeological discoveries are noticed, a surface marker buoy is tied to those objects. Subsequently, its surroundings are explored thoroughly to see if any remains related to it are lying around. Connecting the underwater discoveries or features by rope is useful for all documentation and surveys. Afterwards, a GPS position is obtained for all other purposes followed by excavation and recording. At the end of the survey the marker buoys are removed. In subsequent years the objects are relocated on the basis of the GPS (Global Positioning System) position. Sometimes underwater tags or ropes are left out which help to identify the object during future exploration. It is always suggested to obtain the readings of the GPS at regular intervals for an hour or so and compute the mean value and the mean value could be the accurate position of the site or the discovery.

8. What is underwater probing?

Artefacts lying above the seabed can be easily noticed but not buried artefacts, hence underwater probing is carried out to determine if some are buried in the seabed. Underwater probing is undertaken to determine the extent of artefacts buried in the sediment and to obtain information on the site. Generally probing is undertaken with mild steel rods about 1 m long or smaller, each having a pointed tip at one end and a handle at the other. Probing rods easily penetrate the sediment or seabed but must be handled carefully. While probing, care should be taken that none of the archaeological artefacts such as wood, pottery, ceramic, timber, stone, or metals are damaged (Fig. 31). This survey determines how much overburden is deposited on the artefacts or site.

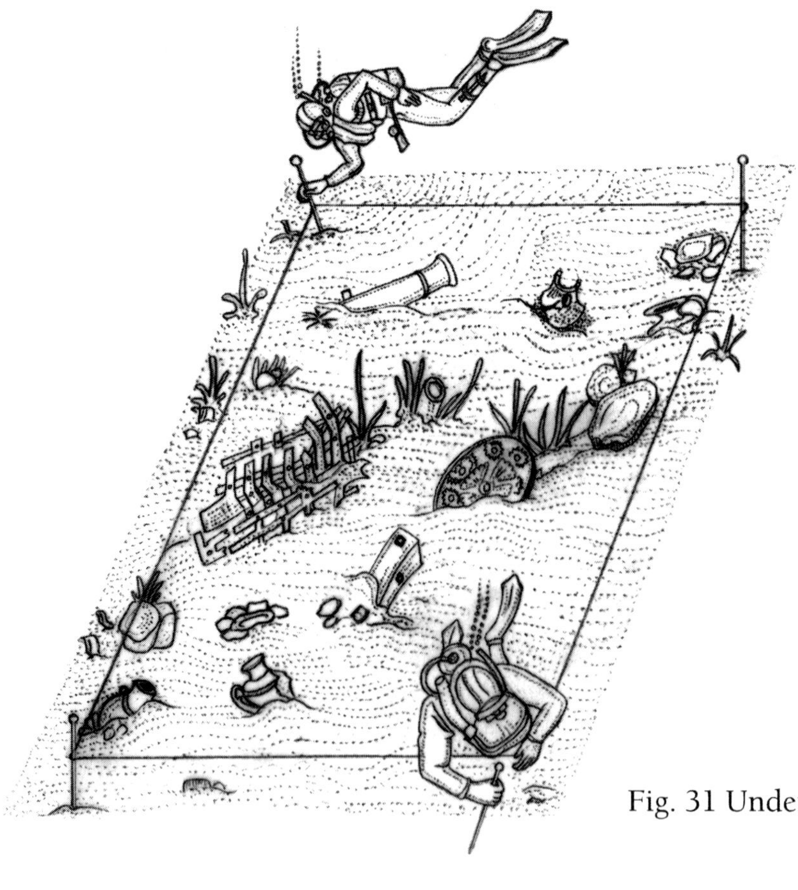

Fig. 31 Underwater probing

9. What is underwater griding?

When recording the excavation finds in open area of the seabed a grid is normally the best system to use. A large or smaller grid is often placed over the site to measure an individual finds or large discoveries and map the site. A grid can be made of aluminium framing or rigid plastic tubing, square in section and non-floating density. Grid helps to obtain an accurate position and precise measurements. It is often found suitable to lay metal grids of 2 m x 2 m squares, over the wrecks, especially if they are on flat sea floors. This allows single divers or pairs of divers to have their own squares in which to excavate, just as on land an archaeologist will have his or her own trench. It can also assist in mapping, especially if the grid is firmly in place and close to the seabed. Some of the underwater structures of Dwarka have been plotted by placing grids (Fig. 32).

Fig. 32 A grid has been laid on the structures in Dwarka waters

10. What are artefacts or objects recovered from the site(s)?

In normal practice nothing should be recovered from a site until properly surveyed, examined and documented. Recovery of objects depends on the objectives of any project. If a number of similar objects such as pottery, stone, bronze or any other metal artefacts are found then some good specimens are recovered for further research and analysis, but only after documentation. On the other hand, most important or valuable artefacts should be recovered after thorough search of surrounding areas and *in situ* documentation. It is always recommended that iron objects should not be lifted unless it is essential. They are among the most complicated to conserve, whereas other metal objects are not so problematic for conservation.

11. How is underwater material lifted?

Divers can carry nylon bags and in the course of exploration bring to the surface in them smaller artefacts which are felt to be important for research. After being studied and documented *in situ*, medium sized and heavy objects are handled manually under water and brought to the surface either by a suitable winch from the boat or by air bags. Air bags of various sizes are available which can be carried deflated to the seabed, attached to a heavy object, and then filled with air to provide buoyancy. Recently, much bigger objects have been lifted by specially designed pontoons. It is always recommended that once artefacts are retrieved from the seabed they be kept in sea water until conservation is started.

12. How are samples collected from underwater sites?

Samples are collected from a site only after experts have identified them for analysis or dating the site and finds. Collection of each type of sample has different procedures; for instance, sediment sample collection varies from rock sample to or wooden sample collections. Care should be taken to avoid contamination of collected samples; soon after collection samples should be kept in either plastic bags or boxes and sealed properly. Each sample should be labelled with full description such as site name, water depth, nature of sample, date, level at which collected etc. The samples should be packed nicely and sent for analysis. Some samples should not be exposed to direct sunlight, hence extra precautions are taken.

CHAPTER EIGHT

SHIPWRECKS

1. What is a shipwreck?

Shipwreck means either sinking or destruction of a ship by any kind of accident either natural or manmade. Shipwrecks occupy a special niche in archaeology. In general terms 'shipwreck' means 'material remains of the ship'. The archaeology of ships called nautical archaeology (from the ancient Greek word for ship '*naus*'), also reveals design and construction details of various types of watercraft, including merchant vessels, warships and fishing boats. Shipwreck study helps us understand the technical achievements and interactions of people in the past. Shipwreck archaeology is a field of historical archaeology as a whole and contains clues to maritime heritage. Shipwreck exploration provides information on maritime history, age of the wreck, cargo, destination, flag of the ship, etc. A shipwreck is a storehouse of knowledge of the history of shipping and navigation.

2. What literary and pictorial evidence is available for shipwrecks in India?

Indian epics namely the *Mahabharata*, the *Puranas*, *Rig Veda*, *Kathasarita Sagar*, and regional legends and traditions refer to shipwrecks. The Buddhist art of Ajanta, Aurangabad and Kanheri in Maharashtra and Ratnagiri in Orissa depicts shipwreck scenes. Buddhist *Jataka* stories and Motupalli pillar inscriptions of Ganapatideva (AD 1244-45) and Annapottu Reddi (AD 1358) of Andhra Pradesh mention shipwrecks. Archival documents as well as marine records kept in various archives and libraries in India and abroad mention shipwrecks in Indian waters. Indian ships wrecked in foreign waters are also mentioned in marine records. The archival records sometime provide information such as the name of ship, destination, captain, port of call, cargo and causes of wreck. Most of the records remain vague about the exact location of the wreck.

3. What are the causes of shipwrecks?

There could be various causes for shipwrecks. These can be divided into two groups: human-related and nature-related causes:

Human-related causes include:

1. Economic - inferior construction, equipment or repair; improper loading, piracy, naval battles, being torpedoed, captured and sabotaged;
2. Seamanship - unskilled navigation, arrogance of captain or crew in navigation or ship-handling, foundering, leaking, capsizing and colliding;
3. Technological - inaccurate charts;
4. Other - fire of unknown origin, etc.

Nature-related causes include:

1. Atmospheric - wind of various degrees from squall to hurricane; and reduced visibility by fog, rain, etc;
2. Oceanic - tides, swells, etc;
3. Climatic - icebergs;
4. Tectonic - earthquake generate tsunami (tidal waves).

4. What happens after the wreck?

Soon after the wreck event all heavy artefacts including the metals will sink and the light materials will float away. Depending upon the importance and value of the artefacts and cargo, sometimes contemporary attempts were made to salvage them. Historical and marine records describe this. Crew and officers onboard die or survive depending on the circumstances of disaster. Over a period of time perishable material will be disintegrated by marine organisms and environmental impact and biofouling will start on the metal objects. Sometimes metal objects are buried in the seabed. The job of the maritime archaeologists comes at last to undertake exploration and excavation of the wreck site.

5. What is the aftermath of shipwreck?

If a ship lands on mud or sand then the chances of the ship and cargoes surviving are greater. However, some may be affected by wave and current actions. The mud piles up against the hull and if the ship sank listing steeply with one side down and the hull pointing in the direction of the fall, the lower side of the ship would very rapidly fill with mud or sand. Anything which lay beneath the mud or sand would be preserved; the state of the hull would be good and corrosion as well as marine growth comparatively less. The chances of survival of shipwrecks are greater in deeper waters. Several deep water shipwrecks have been excavated in different waters of the world. Deeper and colder water simultaneously keeps organisms and human plunderers away from wrecks.

6. What is the importance of shipwreck studies?

The studies of shipwrecks are important in many ways. Any wreck which is older than AD 1800 is a historically important wreck. Hence, study of shipwrecks prior to the 19th century is essential. A shipwreck signifies as a 'time capsule' because the artefact assemblage with it represents one distinct point in time. Thus the study of a shipwreck can reveal the history of the ship, i.e. its construction design, destination, period, port of call, contents and cargo, providing a storehouse of knowledge on the maritime trade and shipping of its time. Lastly, the study reveals the possible reasons for her wrecking. The importance of the study of a shipwreck is further enhanced if the ship was associated with some significant event(s) or person(s).

7. How do maritime archaeologists locate shipwrecks?

Shipwrecks are found in many ways: one way is to search for information in the available records and references. The study of these records provides information on the ship, causes of wreck and sometimes its approximate location. On the basis of available information on shipwrecks explorations are carried out to locate them by deploying different equipment. Sometimes a shipwreck is found accidentally in the course of surveys carried out for some other purpose. After undertaking preliminary exploration of the shipwreck other information on the wreck is collected from records and published sources. Sometimes local fishermen and amateur divers provide information on the location of shipwrecks.

8. How are deep water wrecks more valuable than shallow water wrecks?

Deep sea wrecks offer numerous advantages over shallow water wrecks. Shallow water wrecks are found severely damaged and scattered over a wide area after striking against rocks or reefs, highly effected by environment, encrustations and marine growth, ransacked by non-archaeologists and decayed over the period of time. Deep water wrecks are found intact (less damaged comparatively than shallow water wrecks), less disturbed, not ransacked, less covered by marine growth and encrustations are less, and with artefacts better preserved. Though the exploration of deep water wrecks is highly costly it provides more information on the history of the ship than the shallow water wrecks.

9. How many shipwrecks have so far been located in Indian waters by NIO?

Numerous Indian and foreign ships have been wrecked in India waters, where exploration of shipwrecks was initiated in 1988. So far NIO has explored four shipwrecks (Sunchi Reef, St George's Reef, Amee Shoals and Grande Island) off Goa, four in (Minicoy Island and Suheli Par) off Lakshadweep Islands, and one off Poompuhar in Tamil Nadu waters. Information on several shipwrecks which are yet to be explored has been collected from archival sources and fishermen. Further, several recent period shipwrecks have also been noticed during field trips in different parts of India.

10. What are the difficulties of locating shipwrecks in Indian waters?

Though the archival records indicate several shipwrecks in Indian waters, their exact locations are vague. Rarely are exact positions marked. The rivers of India discharge tons of sediment into the sea and this may have buried a number of shipwrecks including other archaeological artefacts. Poor underwater visibility in shallow water is due to movement of suspended material in many parts of India, and this also makes it difficult to locate shipwrecks. Due to these reasons not many wrecks have so far been explored in Indian waters. Unless the exact locations of shipwrecks are known it becomes difficult to locate them and this is our major concern.

11. What are the findings of shipwrecks in Goa waters?

Explorations off Goa yielded two shipwrecks, namely at Sunchi Reef and St George's Reef and those are datable to the early 17th century and 19th century AD respectively. The findings of Sunchi Reef include the brass barrel of a handgun, iron guns, an iron anchor, a gun shot, Chinese ceramic, sherds of Martaban pottery (stoneware), bases of glass bottles, elephant tusks and hippopotamus teeth, lead pipe, a copper vessel and strip, door knocker, stone and clay bricks and dressed granite stone blocks (Fig. 33). These finds suggest that the Sunchi Reef wreck belonged to the Portuguese Period.

The other wreck explored on St George's Reef belongs to the Basel Mission Company. The shipwreck finds include various types of terracotta artefacts intended for house construction which include a Corinthian column capital, hollow column drum, earthenware, drainage pipes, vases, basins, ridge, roof and floor tiles and chimney bricks (Fig. 34). *Basel Mission Tile works 1865* is

Fig. 33 Artefacts recovered from a shipwreck off Sunchi Reef

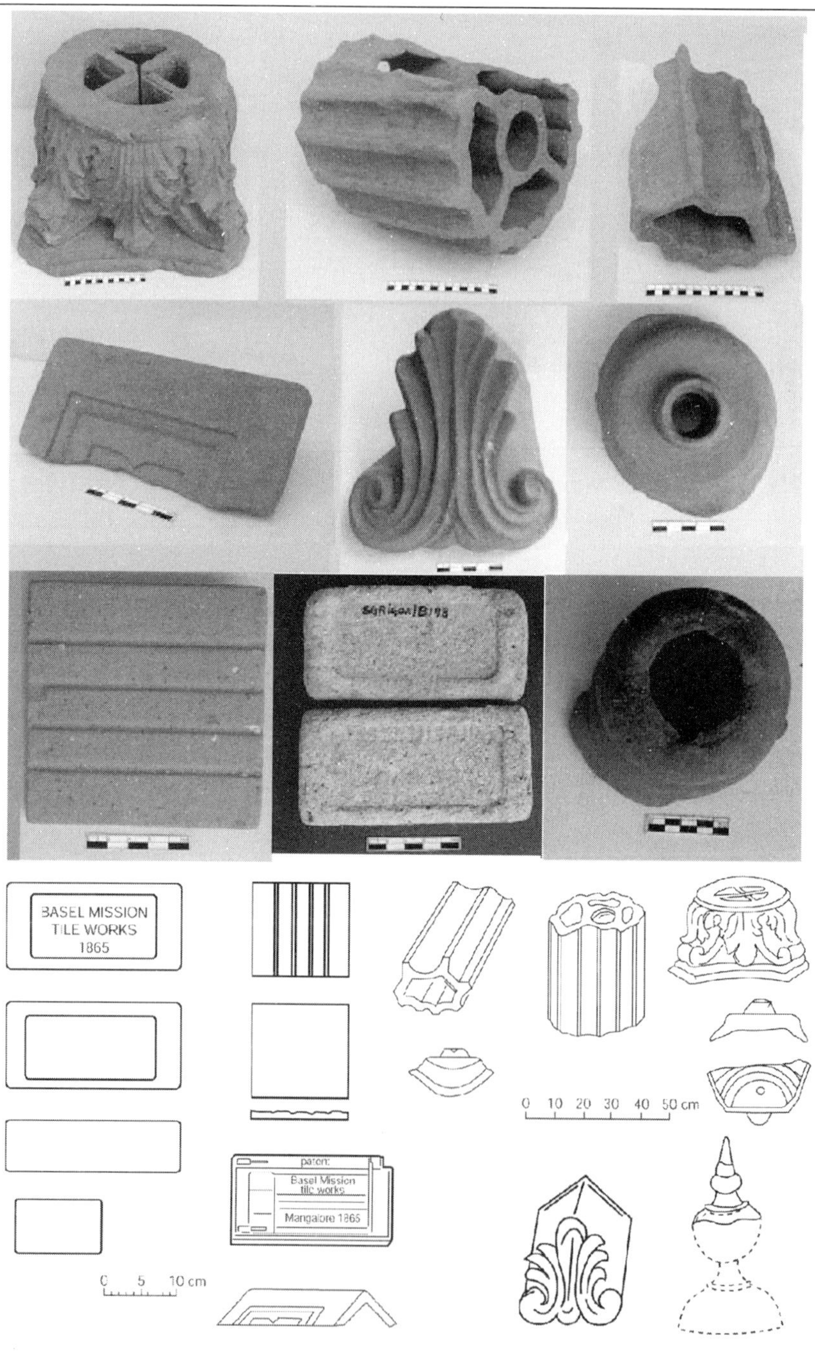

Fig. 34 Types of tiles and other artefacts which have been recovered from a shipwreck off St George's Reef

impressed on chimney bricks and tiles. Study shows that this is the first wreck of the Basel Mission Company located during underwater exploration. On the basis of carbon 14 dating of the timber the wreck could be 115 years old.

The explorations off Grande Island yielded a steel hulled cargo vessel having cabin, hatch and bridge (Fig. 35). These are scattered over a large area. It could be less than a century old. The cabin is ransacked and the lower deck and hull lie covered by thick layer of sand. The mast and ladder are lying on the seabed. It appears that the ship might have sunk in a storm after it lost its anchor and drifted towards the rock near the shore of the island. This wreck site could be the best for imparting training to newcomers.

The exploration off Amee Shoals has brought to light remains of a steam engine shipwreck. The remains of this wreck are scattered over a large area and local divers have salvaged some of its remains. In course of exploration bricks of the boilers, flanges, water tank, brass objects, some copper pipe and cable were collected for further study and analysis. The fly wheel and three boilers are lying close to each other.

Fig. 35 Diver archaeologist examines a shipwreck off Grande Island

12. What are the findings of shipwrecks off Lakshadweep?

Three steam engine shipwrecks were explored in Minicoy waters and one in Suheli Par. All these shipwrecks were documented and belong to the 19th and 20th centuries AD. This period is the transition phase between wood to iron and sail to steam. The Suheli Par Reef shipwreck remains belong to a Greek ship, which was carrying Second World War surplus stores from Burma and ran aground at night in December 1955. During research, information has been collected on a number of steam engine wrecks in Lakshadweep waters. After reopening of the Suez Canal, Lakshadweep played as an important milestone in the shipping route between West Asia and North Africa on one side and South Asia and the Far East on the other. In the absence of lighthouses at Lakshadweep Islands prior to the Second World War many steam engine ships were wrecked because of submerged reefs.

13. What remains were observed off Suheli Par shipwreck?

Suheli Par lies on the international sea route. Offshore exploration in Suheli Par Reef brought to light remains of a wreck which contains a number of armoured vehicles, different types of tyres of various vehicles, trucks, cars and cannon. Explorations were carried out at 6-15 m water depth, but since the sea was choppy, it was not possible to dive close to the reef for thorough examination as well as documentation of the remains of the wreck (Fig. 36). More remains are lying in deep water. It is also not certain whether only one ship was wrecked or more which is yet to be determined.

Fig. 36 Shipwreck remains lying over Suheli Par Reef

14. What remains were observed in the shipwreck off Minicoy?

At the southernmost side of Minicoy Island a steam engine shipwreck was explored and the flywheel and a 27 m long shaft attached to the flywheel and propeller were observed. The most interesting find was an anchor chain running more than 50 m in length with the anchor lying in deeper water. This indicates that the ship was anchored and perhaps drifted to the shore and was wrecked. A few brass and lead pieces were also recorded from this wreck, whose hull frames were still in good condition (Fig. 37). The other wreck is lying perpendicular to the shore, about 200 m north of the previous one. The boilers and engine parts are well preserved. The ship is tilted towards the starboard side. The aft portion of the wreck has fallen into deeper water. The propeller shaft is broken into two parts. A smaller part is attached to the engine but the longer part together with the propeller is broken and has slipped down the slope. Two huge boilers were noted; these are cylindrical with airtight boxes about 5 m in height and 2 m in diameter (Fig. 38).

Fig. 37 Remains of hull, frames and beams of the shipwreck off Minicoy

Fig. 38 Remains of engine, boiler and flywheel of the shipwreck off Minicoy

15. What finds are noticed at shipwreck off Poompuhar, Tamil Nadu coast?

The underwater exploration off Poompuhar, Tamil Nadu yielded an 18th century shipwreck 18 to 19 m deep. A number of lead ingots, copper rudder gudgeon with pins (Fig. 39), copper nails of various sizes, timber from the ship and an iron gun were recorded at the shipwreck site. Four varieties of ingots were recovered; among them a few have a distinct inscription W: BLACKETT, VECI and merchant marks with 1791 and 1792 (Fig. 40). The records of the W: Blackett Company shows that this company was a well known lead exporting company of England from 1694. Lead isotopic analysis revealed the source of the lead ingots to be the North Pennine lead mines of England. Similar types of W: Blackett ingots have been reported from Australia, Netherlands and Sumatra. The wreck off Poompuhar may be a local cargo ship carrying the traded lead ingots of different manufacturers.

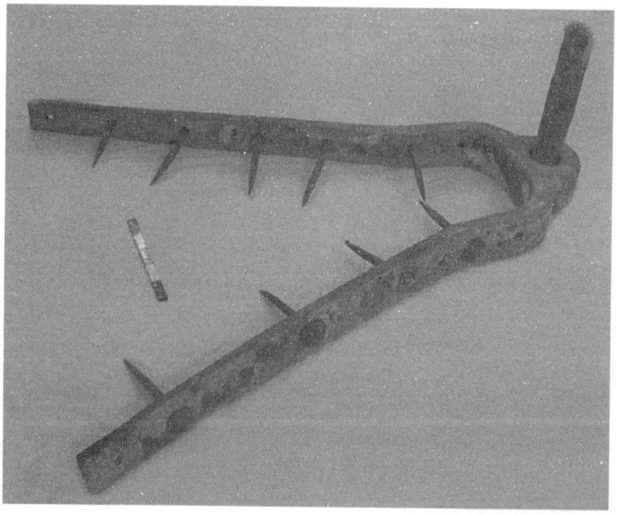

Fig. 39 Rudder gudgeon along with rudder pintle and nails found in the shipwreck off Poompuhar

Fig. 40 Lead ingots lying on the seabed in the shipwreck off Poompuhar

16. What are the possible shipwreck sites where exploration can be carried out in future?

Information on several shipwrecks has been collected in Indian waters on the basis of which preliminary explorations were carried out at Byramogore reef, Lakshadweep to locate a wreck, but its remains are lying in deeper waters. However, some metal pieces have been retrieved which were lying on the reef. The East India Company ship the *DartMouth*, carrying treasure, is said to have sunk off Masulipatnam in 1719, and another ship, the *Governor Keating*, carrying Kings Stores, sank in a storm in 1812 near Nellore, Andhra Pradesh. Attempts are being made to collect further information on these wrecks and exploration can be carried out to locate them. Similarly, archival records state that several Portuguese ships have been wrecked off the Goa coast and attempts have been made to locate and explore them.

17. Has shipwreck research revealed major finds of maritime trade from Goa to the outside world?

The shipwreck findings of Goa shows that ivory and hippopotamus teeth were brought from African countries and were dispatched to Cambay, Surat and other places in Gujarat because artisans concentrated in this region were more skilled than elsewhere. The Portuguese generated huge revenue and wealth by trading with these centres. Ivory was one of their most profitable commodities. They enjoyed a *de facto* monopoly on producing ivory goods and no one could compete with them Besides, ivory and hippopotamus teeth, the type of stone jars and Chinese sherds which have been recovered from Sunchi Reef are similar to the findings of the *Nossa Senhora dos Mártires* (1606) off Lisbon and the *Santo António de Tanná* (1697) off Mombasa, Kenya. It shows that Portuguese ships were engaged in maritime trade in the Indian Ocean, North Atlantic Ocean and South China Sea.

18. Are international historians and scientists interested in study of shipwrecks off Goa?

Yes, shipwreck study requires a multidisciplinary approach. In this kind of research not only have historians taken great interest, but biologists and chemists have shown interest in studying biological and chemical aspects of shipwrecks, whilst engineers and technicians who invent new tools to explore deep water wrecks and others are also involved directly or indirectly. Maritime archaeologists of Australia, South Africa, Portugal, Singapore, Sri Lanka, UK, USA and other countries have shown interest in shipwreck research off Goa. Ideas and discussions on the findings are exchanged in discussions, publications and comparative studies which are found highly useful.

19. Is there any plan to survey shipwrecks off Goa? How many shipwrecks have been identified around Goa that are still unexplored?

Yes, exploration of shipwrecks will be carried out in and around Goa waters and Portuguese trade centres of India in the near future. An attempt has been made to collect information on shipwrecks of this region from the scholars who are involved in this research in Lisbon and other parts of the world. Efforts are made to locate and explore shipwrecks off Goa which are shown on Hydrographic charts. Recently, a shipwreck has been located off Amee Shoals which is marked on the Hydrographic chart and explorations are ongoing. Further, information on steam engine shipwrecks has been collected from Galchibag and Cabo de Rama off Goa waters.

20. How many Indian built ships have been explored in foreign waters?

The marine records which are available in the Archives of Chennai, Mumbai, Delhi, Kolkata, Panaji and other places provide information on the loss of Indian built ships in foreign waters. Maritime archaeologists of other countries have explored and excavated many Indian built shipwrecks. The records state that Indian built ships, namely the *Santo António de Tanná* (1697) built in Thane (near Mumbai), wrecked off Mombasa, Kenya; the *Sydney Cove* and the *Valetta*, which wrecked off Australia, were built in Calcutta (Kolkata). The remains of these wrecks have been studied, making detailed information available. Much more data and information needs to be collected from archives of other countries on Indian built ships wrecked in foreign waters.

21. Which were the unexplored Indian built ships lying in foreign waters?

The *P&O Liner Indus*, which carried the Buddhist sculptures of Bharhut stupa of the 3rd century BC sank in 1882, 50 miles north of Trincomalee in Sri Lankan waters. Similarly, another East India Company ship *Brig Hebe* was wrecked off Colombo in 1852. The East India Company sailing ship *Julius Ceasar* was wrecked off the Maldives Island in 1844 and the *Samarang*, a private passenger ship was lost there in 1849 AD. The marine records mention that the *Bedford* wrecked off Mauritius in 1703. These wrecks should be explored in order to understand the causes of wrecks and find state of the cargo and hull remains.

CHAPTER NINE

CONSERVATION AND DATING METHODS

1. What are post fieldwork processes?

The activities which are carried out after underwater exploration such as cleaning, recording, drawing of findings and conjectural reconstructions, conservation of artefacts, analysis and interpretation of data, comparative study of artefacts with other sites, preparations for report writing and publication are a part of the post fieldwork processes. Explorations are meaningless unless everything is recorded and documented. During the post fieldwork analysis omissions and mistakes and are likely to appear which should not be ignored. The mistakes can be taken care of during future exploration and everyone can learn from them.

2. How are the underwater archaeological artefacts handled and studied?

The artefacts which are found during exploration are recorded under water as far as possible. They are brought to the surface and washed thoroughly in fresh water and if required these are kept in water whilst awaiting the removal of marine deposits and growths. If any artefacts are fragile or in decaying condition the utmost care should be taken to prevent further decay. Chemical treatment and preservatives are applied in consultation with experts, or sometimes experts are invited to undertake the conservation and preservation of artefacts. Subsequently, finds are numbered and catalogued. Before display or storage, the finds are thoroughly analysed and studied. The majority of the finds are drawn with plan, section and elevation and again photographed from various angles if required to be used for reports, displays and publication.

3. How is salt removed from marine artefacts?

The effect of salt can be noticed more on inorganic artefacts (terracotta, ceramics and pottery) than on organic objects. Salt deposits can be removed from such inorganic material by thorough washing and soaking in fresh water for a long time, with the water changed at intervals. These artefacts should first be kept in a 1:1 ratio of sea water and fresh water and the concentration of fresh water should be increased over a period of until the water is basically fresh. Then, after every change of water, salt tests should be conducted for the presence of salt in water. Organic materials, on the other hand, should be kept in sea water for some days. Subsequently 5, 10, 15, 20 % of fresh water is added to them by removing the same quantity of sea water. Desalination continues until all detectable salt has been removed, as shown by salt analyses that estimate the quantity of salt present in the water. On completion of desalination the artefacts should be placed in deionised water, with the solution changed after some intervals.

4. How are underwater artefacts conserved?

Artefacts can be classified into two categories: organic and inorganic. Unless organic material such as bone, leather, rope, wood, ivory is buried safely in the seabed their chances of survival are meagre and they soon perish. After their removal from the seabed these should be either kept in sea water rather than in fresh water till they are conserved scientifically. On the other hand inorganic material such as metal, stone, pottery, glass, ceramic and terracotta artefacts do not deteriorate rapidly underwater. Metal objects should be cleaned neatly in fresh water by adding a little fungicide; cleaning and conservation of each type of metal is different, hence proper attention is required for each metal. Among metals iron requires more attention since it corrodes fast. If a conservator is available it would be his job to adopt various conservation methods for different artefacts. If not, experienced people should be consulted for conservation advice.

5. What is the job of the conservator?

In simple terms the job of the conservator is to preserve artefacts from further decay and disintegration and take care of them. The conservator's task usually includes cleaning, documentation, analysis and finally stabilisation of received artefacts. Wood and other organic materials may be stabilised by freeze drying or by soaking in PEG. PEG, or polyethylene glycol, is a chemical that replaces the water in waterlogged materials, thereby preventing organic such material from shrinking and warping out of recognition as it dries. Sometimes metal artefacts are treated with electrolysis. Finally, preservatives are applied to the objects, which are either displayed or kept in reserve collections. As the finds belong to different categories, each should be dealt with individually and this helps to conserve them properly.

6. What is archaeological conservation of artefacts?

Conservation is the process of preserving archaeological findings so that they may be displayed for and studied for future generations. In the process of conservation no changes should be made to the artefact. The procedure of conservation of organic and inorganic material is different. Conservation deals only with the physical aspect of an artefact and the environmental conditions where it would be displayed or stored. Further, it is essential that a detailed record should be maintained on the work done on the artefact and this would help in future if any problem arises.

7. What are the methods adopted for dating artefacts?

The finds are dated either by absolute or comparative dating methods. Absolute dating methods are highly precise because age is derived by scientific analysis, whereas in the comparative dating method the age is calculated on comparative basis between two or more similar finds from different sites. Both dating methods are acceptable for dating a site or findings. The commonly used absolute dating methods are: (i) carbon-14 dating, (ii) dendrochronology and (iii) thermoluminescence dating. There are a few other dating methods such as oxygen isotope analysis, fission track dating, potassium argon dating, and varve analysis. Various scientific methods are adopted to get the precise date of artefacts. The absolute dating methods used for archaeological purposes are different from the dating methods used for science. Archaeologists use different absolute dating methods depending on the nature and age of an artefact, site or context.

8. What is radiocarbon dating?

The radiocarbon dating method was developed by Dr Walter Libby in 1948. This method is based on measuring the amount of the radioactive carbon isotope, carbon-14 in organic matter. In dead animals and plants the amount declines at a constant rate after death. This method can be used for dating any organic substances up to 50,000 years old. Any organism ceases to absorb carbon after death. 5730 ± 40 years after death half the carbon will be left and after another

5730±40 years half of that amount will remain and this continues for some years. By measuring the amount of radioactivity the age of the organic artefact can be determined with in a range of probability.

9. What is the dendrochronology dating method?

The most accurate and acceptable absolute dating method applied for archaeology is dendrochronology which was developed by A. E. Douglas, University of Arizona in 1929. Dendrochronology is based on counting annual growth rings on trees which regularly add a growth ring each year. During wet years thicker rings are produced whereas dry years yield thinner rings. Over the years distinct and unique patterns of thick and thin rings emerge in the tree. When compared patterns match, each ring corresponds to an exact and known year. This way an old piece of wood can be dated. Matching growth rings in trees helps archaeologists to derive the correct date. The exact date a ship was built can be drawn from a piece of timber of the shipwreck, but it is necessary to find a piece which includes 'sap wood' close to the bark, or else it will be an approximate date.

10. What is thermoluminescence dating method?

Thermoluminescence dating method was developed by Professor Jonson of Dartmouth College in 1964. Thermoluminescence (TL) is the light emitted by a crystalline material while it is undergoing a progressive increase of temperature. The intensity of the light is related to the quantity of ionising radiation to which the material has previously been exposed, and this allows the crystal to be used as a radiation dosimeter. TL can be used in archaeology to date the heating of flint and the exposure of sediments to light when they are deposited. These events cause either a complete removal or a large reduction of the TL that can be emitted from these materials. Consequently, we know that the TL intensity observed at the present day results from the radiation exposure that has occurred since the initial event, and this quantity of radiation can thus be determined. A second set of measurements is then be made to determine the rate at which the radiation dose was delivered to the material by alpha, beta, gamma and cosmic rays which are naturally present. By dividing the total radiation dose by the rate of its delivery, the date of the initial event is obtained.

CHAPTER TEN

INTERNATIONAL SCENARIO

1. What are the foreign countries where maritime archaeological research has been carried out?

The awareness of the preservation of submerged cultural heritage is growing throughout the world. In view of this, maritime archaeological studies have been carried out in Australia, Brazil, Canada, China, Denmark, Egypt, England, France, Germany, Greece, Israel, Italy, Japan, Kenya, Korea, Netherlands, Oman, Philippines, Portugal, Russia, Singapore, South Africa, South America, Spain, Sri Lanka, Sweden, Thailand, Turkey, USA and many other universities and institutes in other countries. These countries have been carrying out the research either with their government organisations or in collaboration with other countries. For instance, Texas A&M University has carried out explorations off Turkey, Florida State University in Egypt and the Western Australian Maritime Museum, has undertaken maritime archaeological studies in Kenya, Korea, Thailand, Sri Lanka, Maldives, Malaysia and Oman.

2. What are the foreign institutes where maritime archaeology courses are taught and degrees offered?

Abroad several colleges and universities are involved in teaching and offering degrees and diplomas in maritime archaeology. The Curtin University of Technology, Flinders University and James Cook University of North Queensland in Australia; East Carolina University in Greenville, North Carolina;

Florida State University, Indiana University, Bloomington, Indiana; and Texas A&M University in the USA; Institute of Archaeology of University College London, University of St. Andrews in Scotland, University of Bristol, University of Oxford, University of Exeter, University of Nottingham and University of Southampton in the UK; and Haifa University, Israel, offer Degrees, Masters, M. Phil and Ph. D on maritime archaeology. The Helsinki University of Finland has the traditional archaeology program. However, there is academic level underwater archaeology. The International Centre for Maritime Archaeology of the Norwegian University of Science and Technology (NTNU) is a leading educational and research institution for Maritime Archaeology; it offers a Master's Degree in Maritime Archaeology and has a Ph. D Program on Maritime Archaeology. There are also a number of societies, which offer courses on maritime archaeology and undertake offshore explorations. Among these societies the Nautical Archaeology Society (NAS), UK is the foremost.

3. When was the Nautical Archaeology Society (NAS) formed and what are its contact details?

NAS was formed in 1981 and established in the UK. People from different countries are associated with NAS and several organisations have collaborated with NAS for underwater archaeological research. NAS involves everyone including divers and non-divers, archaeologists, scientists, historians and others who are interested in promoting underwater archaeology. The society publishes a bi-annual journal the *International Journal of Nautical Archaeology*, the foremost publication in the field of maritime archaeology, and also brings out a regular *Newsletter* for the membership, containing information on expeditions, research news, meetings, conferences and general information. The contact details are: The Nautical Archaeology Society, Fort Cumberland, Fort Cumberland Road, Portsmouth PO4 9LD, UK. The other details of NAS are available on www.nasportsmouth.org.uk

4. What syllabus is included in the NAS course?

NAS has devised a three-part system of certification course in underwater archaeological techniques. Among them part -1 syllabus deals with introductory course which is for archaeologists and divers. This syllabus includes: (i) background and explanation of archaeology, (ii) infrastructure and relevant legislation, (iii) basic principles of archaeology, (iv) basic techniques used in underwater archaeology. NAS conducted Part -1 course at NIO, Goa in 1990 in five days duration in which all the maritime archaeologists of NIO participated.

5. What is the role of Institute of Nautical Archaeology (INA) for the progress of maritime archaeology?

INA was founded in 1973, since then it has expanded its scope and activities to work globally on shipwrecks, submerged and other archaeological sites. All the members of the INA such as professional archaeologists, students and many others from all over the world, united together in their passion for locating and exploring lost ships and submerged sites and applying modern tools and techniques and studying them to unlock their secrets. INA has worked on the world's oldest known shipwrecks and as recent as the World War II. INA archaeologists, students and divers have discovered the first ancient ship with sonar survey and the first to map the seabed with accuracy by means of their own techniques, they are the first to excavate a wreck using saturation diving, and set a record for any underwater project undertaken with compressed-air equipment with their thousand of dives to between 145 and 200 feet at Uluburun, Turkey. By affiliating with Texas A&M University, INA has carried out underwater explorations not only in the United States, but in Spain, Israel, Bulgaria, Jamaica, Japan, Portugal and Egypt and trained the state archaeologists around the world and students from Peru, China, Jamaica, Canada, Belgium, Denmark, Greece, Japan, England, South Africa, Switzerland, Turkey, France, Albania, and other lands.

6. What is the international status of maritime archaeology?

All the developed and a few developing countries have made good progress in maritime archaeological studies by locating and excavating some important shipwrecks like the *Mary Rose*, the *Wasa*, the *Titanic*, the *Amsterdam*, the *Uluburun*, the *Cape Gelidonya*, the *Vergulde Draeck*, the *Batavia*, and submerged ports and habitational sites. Commendable work was done by locating and excavating the *Mary Rose*, warship of King Henry VIII, which was built in AD 1510-11 and sank in 1545. The hull was raised in 1982. A trust was formed in 1967 for retrieving the ship, which has been declared a monument. The *Wasa*, the Swedish man-of-war, which sank in AD 1628, was retrieved in AD 1961. Off the Turkish coast, the *Uluburun* wreck belonging to the late Bronze Age (14th century BC) has been excavated in 60 m water depth. The Portuguese ship the *Santo Antonio de Tanna* (1697) built in Thane (Maharashtra, India), which sank off the Mombasa coast of East Africa, is being salvaged. The other ships being salvaged are the *Nossa Senhora dos Martires* (1606) wrecked off Lisbon, Portugal, and the 18th century *Sydney Cove* built in Calcutta which sank off the Australian coast. The Dutch East India Company ship the *Avondster*, which was wrecked on 2 July

1659 near the Black Fort, Sri Lanka, is also being salvaged. The early 1960s explorations off Great Basses reef of southern Sri Lanka brought to light remains of a wreck and the finds include 350 pounds of silver coins minted in Surat, Gujarat, west coast of India, a British bronze cannon and flintlock pistols and the ship may have been built in Southeast Asia. These silver coins belong to the Mughal Empire Muhammad Aurangzeb Alamgir (1658-1707), with Islamic date 1113 AH. Such shipwreck excavations have enhanced knowledge of the history of seafaring of mankind and has inspired new directions for future research.

7. Who were the scholars, who contributed to the growth of maritime archaeology in other parts of the world?

Professor George Bass and his team have worked in the Mediterranean sea along the Turkish coast and in Cyprus; Honor Frost has worked along the Turkish and Lebanese coast; Professor Cheryl Ward of Florida State University has worked in Egypt; Professor Sean McGrail and his team of Southampton University, UK, have worked in India and Bangladesh; Robin Piercy of INA worked in Mombasa, Kenya; Professor Jeremy Green and his team from the Western Australian Maritime Museum have carried out explorations off Southeast Asian countries, Oman and Sri Lanka; Professor Avner Raban of Haifa University, Israel, worked in the Red Sea and Greece; and Robert Parthesius and his team from the Netherlands worked in Sri Lanka. These are a few maritime archaeologists who have also directly or indirectly contributed immensely to the growth of maritime archaeology.

8. Who were foreign scholars immensely helped in the progress of maritime archaeology?

Among the maritime archaeologists of the world Professor George F. Bass holds a high respect and dignity in this field and is also the founder of the Institute of Nautical Archaeology, with a Research Centre in Bodrum, Turkey. He has explored a number of Bronze Age and later shipwrecks in the Mediterranean Sea. Honor Frost has worked extensively on the stone anchors of the Mediterranean Sea, Red Sea and Punic warships off Sicily. Jeremy Green of AIMA, Australia, has carried out extensive explorations in Korea, Malaysia, Maldives, Sri Lanka and Thailand. Ole Crumlin-Pedersen has excavated five Viking ships in Denmark's Roskilde Fjord in 1962 and set up a research institute at Roskilde which is a world leader in maritime archaeological research today. Other maritime archaeologists are Peter Throckmorton, Joan du Plat Taylor, Honor Frost, Nic Flemming, A. J. Parker, Colin Martin, Richard Gould, Michael Katzev, Daniel J. Lenihan, James

Delgado, Sean McGrail, Robert Grenier, Eric Rieth, Cemal Pulak, Chris Dobbs, Keith Muckelroy, Michael L'hour, Avner Raban, Francisco Alves, Robin Piercy, Jean Y. Blot, Filipe Castro, Cheryl Ward, Gerhard Kapitan, Myra Stanbury, Mack McCarthy, Jonathan Adams, Johan Ronnby, Alessandra Nibbi, Lucy Blue, Michael Flecker, Thijs Maarleveld, Mike Nash, Mark Staniforth, Paul Brandt, Somasiri Devendra, Bruno Werz, Valerie Feriwick, Paula Martin, Graeme Henderson, Martin Dean, Robert D. Ballard, Dionisius Agius, David Nutley, Harry Tzalas, Jeo Flatman, Masaaki Kimura, Sarah Arenson and many others who have contributed immensely to the progress of maritime archaeology.

9. Which are the submerged habitation sites of the world?

There is an increasing amount of evidence for submerged landscapes. Several submerged prehistoric sites have been discovered in Australia, Japan, North America, South Africa and many European countries; Palaeolithic stone tools such as hand axes and choppers, bones, food remains and cut timbers have been recovered. Similarly, a submerged prehistoric site has been located in the Little Salt Spring in southwest Florida, USA datable to 12,000 BP. Thousands of Mesolithic settlements have been explored in the Baltic Sea and the finds include burials, wood, antlers, flint tools, bone artefacts and canoes. A pre-pottery Neolithic site datable to the 7th millennium BC has been located at Atlit off the coast of Israel near Haifa from where human burials, house foundations, animal and fish bones, flint and stone tools have been recovered. In comparison with the north Mediterranean coast the rate of discovery of habitational submerged sites in the rest of the world is proportionately less because a great deal of diving and underwater archaeological exploration have been ongoing along the coast of the Mediterranean Sea. The submerged land in the North Sea between Britain and Denmark is known as 'Doggerland'.

10. How was Port Royal, Jamaica submerged and what was found?

One of the most shocking events in the history of mankind was the disastrous earthquake on 7th June 1692 at Port Royal, Jamaica. It is estimated that in 1692 the number of residents in Port Royal could have been approximately 8,000 and comprised residents, merchants, ship captains, craftsmen, slaves and pirates. The strong earthquake sank two-thirds of the city in Kingston harbour. Underwater investigations were carried out by INA from 1960 to 1990 and thousands of artefacts were recovered, including brass, copper, silver and pewter metal objects, Chinese porcelain, iron tools, glass bottles and building remains. Surprisingly, the exploration also led to the recovery of a British warship *HMS Swan* lying buried among the building debris.

11. What are the submerged port sites of the world?

In antiquity most ports were located on river estuaries and in the case of lagoons at outlets to the sea, where vessels could find refuge. In the establishment of ports the geographical considerations of the region had to be taken into account. In addition to this maritime structure like boatbuilding sites, landing places, boat shelters, wharfs, jetties, breakwaters and moorings played a vital role in the establishment of ports. These features have been encountered during excavations in Denmark, Egypt, Finland, Sweden and other countries, dating from the Bronze Age to the 20th century. Evidence of the remains of harbours has been noticed in the Mediterranean Sea particularly at Arwad, Sidon and Tyre. Remains of massive sea walls can be seen at the harbour site at Arwad. Probably a warehouse and jetty have been located at Sidon. It is noticed that the northern shores of the Mediterranean Sea are generally more rocky than the southern and so there are many more sheltered bays, which served as anchorages from the earliest times. Intensive surveys have been carried out to locate harbours in many parts of the Mediterranean Sea including Apollonia in Libya, Athlit in Israel, Cosa in Italy, Phaselis in Turkey and Kenchreai and Porto Cheli in Greece.

12. How did UNESCO come into the picture of maritime archaeology?

The advent of scuba diving gear had a major impact on the underwater sites of the world. More and more sites were looted and destroyed by treasure hunters before archaeologists and academics developed an interest in the study of the underwater heritage. The treasure hunters of the Caribbean region were destroying valuable sites in spite of bureaucratic opposition to the process. With passage of time the rapid growth of treasure hunting became a major concern for governments and archaeologists. A number of sites off the Mediterranean coast were ransacked and looted before the United Nations Educational, Scientific and Cultural Organization (UNESCO) came forward. In November 2001 the Convention on the Protection of Underwater Cultural Heritage was adopted by the Plenary session of the 31st General conference which was also the UNESCO's Fourth Heritage Convention. The UNECSO Convention proposed strict guidelines for the preservation of underwater heritage. The General conference emphasizes an international desire that underwater cultural heritage should be protected.

13. In what way is UNESCO concerned with maritime archaeology?

In UNESCO maritime archaeology comes under the purview of 'underwater cultural heritage'. The underwater cultural heritage (UCH) has been defined as all traces of human existence lying on the seabed, riverbeds, or at the bottom of lakes. It includes: material of a cultural, historical or archaeological character and other objects such as sites, structures, buildings, and artefacts which have lain under water for at least 100 years; other sites of prehistoric date, sunken towns and ancient ports which were once on the land and then submerged due to climatic or geological changes. It is UNESCO's aim that all objects of an archaeological and historical nature found on the seabed should be preserved for the benefit of mankind as a whole. The main concern is that the technological advances in scuba diving since World War II and the increasing interest in underwater exploration for both recreational and commercial purposes pose a severe threat to the preservation of cultural and historical resources.

In view of this UNESCO is taking all practicable measures to increase public awareness of the value and significance of the underwater cultural heritage and the importance of its protection. In this regard UNESCO proposes that academic institutes and universities should undertake training programmes on underwater archaeology, particularly in developing countries, and sees this as of great importance. Further, UNESCO suggests the establishment of a standardized curriculum and setting up of practical training on wreck sites to provide improved field training for underwater archaeologists.

14. What is the future of maritime archaeology in a global context?

Often the best way to gauge future development is to examine the recent past. Maritime archaeology has always been dependent on technology for the simple reason that human beings lack gills and can do no more than grab objects from the seabed. Having said that sponge divers have played an important part in locating historic shipwrecks and reporting them to archaeologists, while ancient harbours and crannogs in shallow water have been surveyed with no need for diving equipment. Now that scuba equipment is available to everyone, countries with vulnerable underwater sites have had to ban recreational diving in an effort to prevent looting. Legislation prohibiting the sale of antiquities has been introduced to protect both land and underwater sites. In many places this has come too late; most shipwreck sites in coastal waters have already been destroyed by indiscriminate pillage and there continues to be an international black market in antiquities. Despite the 2001 UNESCO Convention on the Protection of the Underwater Cultural Heritage, treasure salvors continue to operate in many parts of the world. As a mitigating strategy, some poor countries license treasure salvage in exchange for a percentage of finds, but the Convention rules out such compromises by professional archaeologists.

The future will see a continuing struggle to prevent pillaging of the underwater heritage by both individuals and consortia. Meanwhile coastal development and bottom dredging by trawlers is destroying maritime archaeological information on an unprecedented scale. Rescue interventions will continue to be a priority for maritime archaeologists everywhere.

15. What is the potential for maritime archaeology in a global context?

The seas and oceans connect the countries of the world and maritime archaeology is well placed to foster international cooperation, for ships are often wrecked in distant waters and carry cargoes from foreign lands. The future holds out both challenges and rewards for coming generations of maritime archaeologists. Coastal development and extraction of marine minerals will continue to provide marvellous opportunities to access deeply buried deposits where there are ancient land surfaces. Here may be found superbly preserved organic artefacts and habitation sites which do not survive on dry land. Thus Mesolithic paddles from Tidbrind Vig, Denmark still bear painted decoration, while metro and tunnel construction in Olbia, Sardinia; Pisa, Italy and Istanbul, Turkey have uncovered ancient harbours full of ship remains. Increasingly sophisticated remote sensing devices enable archaeological sites to be assessed without intervention and computer enhanced photogrammetry and mosaic photography make possible the survey of deepwater wreck sites.

SUGGESTED READING

- Barker, P., 1986. *Understanding Archaeological Excavation*. Batsford, London.
- Bass, G. F., 1966. *Archaeology Under Water*. Praeger Publishers, New York.
- Bass, G. F., (Ed.) 2005. *Beneath the Seven Seas*. Thames & Hudson, London.
- Dean, M., *et. al.*, 1995. *Archaeology Underwater*. Nautical Archaeology Society, London.
- Dean, M., 1988. *Guidelines on acceptable standard in underwater archaeology*. The Scottish Maritime Studies Development Association.
- Delgado, J, P., (Ed.) 1997. *Encyclopaedia of Underwater Maritime Archaeology*. British Museum Press, London.
- Gibbins, D., and Adams, J., (Eds.) 2001. Shipwrecks. *World Archaeology*, Vol. 32 (3): 279-432.
- Gibbins, D., 1990. Analytical approaches in maritime archaeology: a Mediterranean perspective. *Antiquity*, Vol. 64: 376-389.
- Gifford, J, A., *et al.*, 1985. The Unesco International survey of underwater cultural heritage. *World Archaeology*, Vol. 16 (3): 373-376.
- Graver, D., 1984. *Padi Diver Manual*. PADI, California.

- Green, J., 2004. *Maritime Archaeology: A Technical Handbook*. Elsevier Academic Press, Amsterdam.
- Greenhill, B., 1995. The *Archaeology of Boats and Ships an Introduction*. Conway Maritime Press, London.
- Griffith, N., Jenner, A., and Wilson, C., 1990. *Drawing Archaeological Finds, A Handbook*. Archetype Publications, London.
- Illsley, J. S., (Ed.) 1996. *An Indexed Bibliography of Underwater Archaeology and Related Topics*. Anthony Nelson, Shropshire.
- Joiner, J. T., 2001. *NOAA Diving Manual, Diving for Science and Technology*. Best Publishing Company, Flagstaff AZ, USA.
- Joint Nautical Archaeology Policy Committee 1989. *Heritage at Sea: Proposals for the better protection of archaeological sites underwater*. National Maritime Museum, London.
- Lockery, A., 1985. *Marine Archaeology and the Diver*. Ontario, Canada.
- Martin, C. J., *et al.*, 1981. *Protection of the underwater heritage, Protection of the cultural heritage technical handbooks for museums and monuments 4*. UNESCO, Paris.
- McGrail, S., (Ed.) 1984. *Aspects of Maritime Archaeology and Ethnology*. National Maritime Museum, London.
- Muckelroy, K., 1978. *Maritime Archaeology*. Cambridge University Press, Cambridge.
- Orser, C. E., (Ed.) 2002. *Encyclopaedia of Historical Archaeology*. London.
- Renfrew, C., and Bahn, P., 1991. *Archaeology: Theories, methods and practice*. Thames & Hudson, London.
- Robinson, W., 1998. *First Aid for Underwater Finds*. Archetype Publications & NAS, London.
- Ruppe, C. V., and Barstad, J. F., (Eds.) 2002. *International Handbook of Underwater Archaeology*. Kluwer Academic/ Plenum Publishers, New York.
- Throckmorton, P., (Ed.), 1987. *History from the Sea: Shipwrecks and Archaeology*. Mitchell Beazley International Ltd., London.

- UNESCO, 1972. *Underwater Archaeology: a nascent discipline*. UNESCO, Paris.
- UNESCO, 1981. *Protection of the Underwater Heritage*. UNESCO, Paris.

AN INTRODUCTION TO MARITIME ARCHAEOLOGICAL EXPLORATIONS IN INDIAN WATERS

Dwarka

Situated on the Arabian Sea coast, Dwarka (Jamnagar district) is an important religious place for Hindus. According to scriptures Dwarka was associated with Lord Krishna and was submerged soon after his departure to his heavenly abode. Noted historian Pargiter (1904 and 1922) suggested that Dwarka was located near the Raivataka Mountain and that it was constructed on the remains of Kusasthali. Similarly, Pusalkar (1943 and 1945) accepted that modern Dwarka was the original Dwarka of the *Mahabharata*. However, many scholars have identified different places in Gujarat as the original Dwarka.

Offshore exploration was initiated in 1982-83 and led to the recovery of a large number of dressed semicircular and rectangular stone blocks and structures. Some of the stone blocks have an L-shape and have provision for dowels. A few stone blocks and structures still retain the hard cementing material that had bonded them. These structures have 2 to 3 courses of 60 to 80 cm height the average size 95 × 55 × 25 cm. The stone blocks could have belonged to a jetty, which might have collapsed over the years. Structures similar to these have also been noticed in the intertidal zone of Rupen Bandar, 3 km north of Dwarka. The Rupen Bandar stone structures belong to a jetty which was datable to the 20th century. However, the Dwarka structures are older to Rupen Bandar: some of the blocks lie on the rocky seabed and a few are buried in sand. Exposed stone blocks are covered with a thick growth of seaweeds and a pinkish layer of marine growth. The discovery of modern Gujarati script on one rectangular stone block suggests that these stone blocks may not be very old. Further, geophysical survey delineated the ancient channel of the River Gomati over a length of 1.2 km seaward at 8 to 10 m water depth (Vora *et al*. 1991).

In the course of underwater exploration iron anchors, copper *lotas*, and pieces of marble statue (sometimes a foot along with the pedestal and a palm and a female statue) have been recovered that may belong to the early medieval period. A number of brass objects such as a bell, pins, flat rectangular bars and 'U'- shaped bars with perforations and a smaller size rudder gudgeon have also been retrieved from Dwarka waters. These brass objects appear to belong to a boat.

The discovery of varieties of stone anchors in Dwarka waters is worth mentioning. These are mostly made of limestone and sandstone and are similar in form to anchors found in the coastal waters of Oman and east African, Sri Lanka, Maldives, Tamil Nadu, Goa, Maharashtra, Kerala and Minicoy in the context of the early to the late medieval period. Evidently, the finding of stone anchors indicates that Dwarka was a very active port during the medieval period. All this suggests that anchors from Dwarka may be dated to between the 9th and 17th centuries AD.

Moreover, investigations both near shore and offshore have so far not revealed any pottery, artefacts and other antiquities belonging to the protohistoric period. Explorations has been carried out from shallow water to 25 m water depth, but so far no remains of any submerged of ancient settlement were found. Even though all the underwater findings of Dwarka were earlier dated to 1500 BC on a comparative basis, it is now clear that none of the underwater explorations yielded any artefacts or objects which can be dated scientifically to the *Mahabharata* period.

Bet Dwarka

Bet Dwarka Island, also known as Bet Shankhodhara, is situated in the Gulf of Kachchh, 30 km north of Dwarka. NIO has carried out onshore and intertidal zone explorations there. Discoveries confirm that the island was occupied from the protohistoric period (4000 years BP) to date. The findings include a Harappan type seal, graffiti on three potsherds, a copper fish hook, pottery, terracotta and fish bone beads and shell bangles belong to centuries soon after the Harappa Civilisation. Early historic settlement remains have been located on the island which may date back to the 3rd century BC. A potsherd is inscribed with '*Nandakasa*' in the Mauryan Brahmi script and there are also Kushana coins. A medieval iron cannon and Mughal period coins have also been collected from the island. A site was noticed near *Khuda Dargha*, submerged during high tide, and this suggests that some changes in shoreline and sea level occurred after the Christian era.

Offshore exploration on the northern side of present Bet Dwarka jetty brought to light a number of stone anchors similar to the Dwarka finds. These anchors are made of locally available rocks and the period of these anchors may be the same as those of Dwarka and other sites in India. The recent underwater exploration at the same site have brought to light sherds of amphorae, lead ingots, and lead anchors which are assignable to the early centuries of the Christian era and emphasize the existence of maritime trade with the Roman world.

Somnath

Like Dwarka, Somnath (Prabhasa) is a holy place of historic importance. Somnath is mentioned in the *Mahabharata* as *Prabhasatirtha* and the *Bhagawata Purana* says that at this sacred place the River Saraswati flows towards the west and the town is situated on the seashore. The Nasik and Karle cave inscriptions of Nahapana (AD 119-124) also refer to Prabhasa.

Prabhasa, which seems to have extended up to Somnath, was a port during the protohistoric period. The excavations at Prabhasa brought to light what could be a warehouse on the bank of the River Hiran (Hiranya). This identification was made because the building appears to have been unroofed (Dhavalikar 1977-78). Onshore and nearshore exploration at Somnath were carried out in 1991 and brought to light Late Harappan pottery and Red Polished ware (RPW) in and around the excavated area and on the bank of River Hiran.

Offshore exploration covering an area of almost 500 × 500 m was carried out southwest of Somnath Temple. The seabed is rocky. A large number of stone anchors were found very similar to those from Dwarka and Bet Dwarka.

The offshore explorations off Somnath brought to light ring stone, and anchors of composite and Indo-Arabian type similar to those found at Dwarka and Bet Dwarka, dressed stone blocks, and rock cut channels (Rao, Sila Tripati and Gaur 1992). Somnath has yielded more ring stone anchors than other sites in India (Gaur *et al*. 2002). However, exploration in Somnath waters so far have not yielded any submerged habitation.

Saurashtra coast

Offshore exploration was carried out along the Saurashtra coast to locate and identify ports and anchorages. In view of this, underwater investigation off Miyani

(*Harshad Mata*) and Kindari Creek, Visawada (Mul Dwarka) were carried out and a number of stone anchors were found. Some of them have been retrieved for study and research. These anchors are similar to those from Dwarka, Bet Dwarka and Somnath. The finds in these regions indicate that Miyani and Mul Dwarka were ports during the early medieval to late medieval period. The unearthing of types of stone anchors also suggests that the mouths of creeks have been widely used as anchorages.

Vijaydurg

Historical records show that frequent naval battles were fought at Vijaydurg by the British and the Marathas. A number of ships were either sunk or burnt down in Vijaydurg waters following an exchange of fire. The foremost objective of underwater exploration and excavation off Vijaydurg waters is to locate shipwrecks.

Diving, airlifting and metal detector surveys were carried out in Vaghotan creek and on the western side of the Vijaydurg Fort in 8 to 10 m of water. The offshore exploration in Vijaydurg waters revealed a structure on the western side of the fort. The structure extends E-W and has an N-S turn. It measures 122 m in length, 7 m width and 3 m height. Different sizes of stone blocks have been used for the construction. Probably the structure was built for the protection of the fort from enemy ships as well as from wave and current action. The finding of Indo-Arabian and composite stone anchors along the Vijaydurg and Sindhudurg coast shed new light on the date of the stone anchors of India. A tidal dockyard measuring 108 m long and 69 m wide was found on the riverbank of Vaghotan. Its entrance is 7 m wide made of dry stone masonry. A rectangular platform had been constructed at the centre of the dock to carry out repair of vessels.

Goa

Maritime archaeological explorations have been initiated in Goa waters for locating port installations and shipwrecks along riverbanks and in coastal waters. Underwater exploration has been carried out in Sunchi Reef, St George's Reef, Amee Shoals, Baga, Grande Island and Aguada waters to locate shipwrecks.

Exploration off Sunchi Reef, around 2 km distant from Marmagao port, has revealed the remains of a shipwreck at 3 to 6 m depth. The important finds include the barrel of a hand gun, Chinese ceramics, sherds of Martaban pottery (stone ware), elephant tusks and hippopotamus teeth, a number of dressed granite blocks, four iron guns - each 2 m long, a cast iron cannon ball, lead pieces, a copper vessel and strip, stone and clay bricks, pieces of glass bottles and a door knocker. Granite blocks and guns are overgrown with barnacles and other sea organisms. These discoveries suggest that the ship arrived in Goa from Portugal via Africa and was grounded due to lack of knowledge of the topography of the coast. Thermoluminescence dating of the pottery suggests that the wreck belonged to the early 17th century AD. The shipwreck finds show the evidence of Indo-Portuguese trade and commerce.

Another shipwreck was explored in 15 m water depth in St George's Reef, on the eastern side of Grande Island. The finds include: various types of artefacts such as inscribed chimney bricks; roof, ridge and floor tiles, the latter being the most numerous; a Corinthian capital for a column; and a drum. The bricks are made of white clay, moulded and inscribed, '*Basel Mission Tile Works 1865*' on the obverse; the reverse is plain. Some of the floor tiles are stamped like the bricks on the reverse and have four deep grooves whereas the obverse is plain. The Corinthian type of capital is hollow inside and one end is closed. A piece of timber, perhaps part of the ship's keel, was also noticed in between the rocks. The C14 dating of the timber suggests that the St George's Reef wreck is about 115 years old and shipwreck therefore occurred in the latter part of the 19th century. The Basel Mission Company had tile factories around Mangalore on the west coast, which exported the products to East Africa, Aden, Basara, Australia and Southeast Asian countries.

In the course of exploration off Amee Shoals three shipwrecks were found. Out of three shipwrecks it appears that one is a steam engine wreck and two others are barges. As the remains of these wrecks are scattered in a large area it is difficult to state which part of a ship belongs to which shipwreck. The engines of the barges have probably been salvaged, whereas the frames and hull remains are lying under water. Similarly the local divers have salvaged some remains from the steam engine wreck. In the course of exploration boiler bricks, a fly wheel, boilers of the engine, flanges, brass objects and some copper pipe pieces were collected for study. The underwater metal detector survey followed by diving in Baga waters has revealed a steel hulled wreck in 5 to 6 m deep water (opposite the seminary). The wreck is buried in the sediment, but a small part is visible.

Further, underwater explorations brought to light Indo-Arabian and ring stone type of stone anchors from Sunchi Reef, Grande Island and Baga waters and a number of iron anchors have been retrieved from the Aguada waters. The wreck sites of Sunchi Reef, St George's Reef and Amee Shoals and the artefacts retrieved from these places provide clinching proof that Goa waters offer a rich potential for shipwreck archaeology.

Lakshadweep

The Lakshadweep Islands lie on the sea route between Africa to the west and South Asia and Southeast Asia on the east. Before the opening of the Suez Canal Lakshadweep was an important halt on the shipping route to take on fresh water. Many of the reefs are very shallow and some of them permanently submerged and were hazardous for mariners. Thus there were many wrecks in the region.

During exploration in Lakshadweep waters four steam engine shipwrecks were found. The first shipwreck was observed lying over Suheli Par Reef, where a major portion can be seen. A Greek ship was carrying a number of armoured vehicles, cars and guns Second World War surplus stores, from Burma and was grounded at night in December 1955. The other three wrecks were found off Minicoy on the western side of the island. A small portion of each wreck was visible above the water. The wrecks were lying in depths of 4 to 15 m.

Diving at one of the southernmost wrecks off Minicoy suggests that this was a steel hulled, steam engine ship. The flywheel was intact and a 27 m long shaft attached to the flywheel and propeller were noted. The most interesting discovery was an anchor chain running more than 50 m, with the anchor lying in deeper water. This indicates that the ship was anchored and perhaps drifted to the shore and was wrecked. A few brass and lead pieces were observed and the hull frame of this wreck is still in good condition.

The other wreck is lying perpendicular to the shore, about 200 m north of the previous one. It is estimated that the length of the ship was 100 m. The boilers and engine parts are well preserved. The ship lists towards the starboard side. The aft portion of the wreck has fallen in deeper water. The propeller shaft is broken into two parts; a small part is attached to the engine but the longer part together with the propeller is broken and has slipped down the slope. Two huge boilers were observed. These are cylindrical and airtight boxes about 5 m in height and 2 m in diameter.

Poompuhar

Poompuhar, known as Kaveripattinam, is one of the most notable ancient Chola ports and is located at the confluence of the River Kaveri and the Bay of Bengal. The Sangam period Tamil epic *Manimekhalai* mentions that the Chola king had lost his son and in his grief omitted to celebrate the annual Indra festival. This enraged the goddess Manimekhalai who caused the city to be swallowed up by the sea. This may be an echo of an actual catastrophe when a high tidal wave engulfed the city.

Offshore exploration opposite the mouth of the River Kaveri brought to light stone structures. Airlifting was carried out extensively off Poompuhar at different water depths and yielded brickbats, red ware, Black and Red ware and some courses of dressed blocks, both square and rectangular. The blocks are highly eroded and no trace of mortar was noticed on them. Similarly, to the north of Poompuhar, a lot of pottery of similar types was found. This evidence indicates that a part of the ancient city was submerged in the sea; the remains are lying at about 8 m water depth.

About 3.5 km off Poompuhar a shipwreck was discovered at a water depth of 19 m, a major portion of which is buried under sediment. A metal detector survey suggested its maximum length and width could be 50 and 15 m. Airlift operations have shown that the ship was wooden hulled. The exploration of the shipwreck brought to light a large number of lead ingots which are classified into four types: (i) Long oval boat-shaped ingots with an inscription W: BLACKETT on one side and the dates 1791 and 1792 on the reverse, (ii) Long oval shaped with a D below a crown symbol and a smaller crown symbol on the reverse along with other symbols, (iii) Square-ended, flat bottomed ingots without inscription or symbol on obverse while on the reverse VEIC inside a heart, (iv) Round ended, semi-circular bottom, boat-shaped ingots without any inscription or symbol on the obverse and a heart symbol stamped on the reverse. Besides the lead ingots, a 2.1 m long iron cannon, gun-powder boxes and a copper rudder gudgeon were also noted. After airlifting it was observed that copper and copper nails of various sizes were extensively used in the construction of the ship. The exposed timber has been highly affected by teredo (woodborers). There are no records to ascertain the country of origin of the ship. The records of the W: Blackett Company shows that this company was a well-known lead exporting company in England since 1694. Lead isotope analysis revealed the source of the lead ingots to be the North Pennine lead mines of England. Similar types of W: Blackett ingots have been reported from Australia, Netherlands and Sumatra. The wreck off Poompuhar may be a local cargo ship carrying the traded lead ingots of different manufacturers. If the ship had a foreign origin, the size would have been much larger because during the 18th and early 19th century steam ships were plying. However, the ill-fated ship is very small in size.

Mahabalipuram

Underwater explorations were carried out off Mahabalipuram to locate archaeological remains. These investigations were carried at several locations in 5 to 8 m water depths 500 to 700 m off the shore temple. Investigations at each location have brought to light wall-like structures, a big square cut rock, scattered square and rectangular stone blocks. Most of the structures are damaged and scattered over a vast area, providing a substratum for barnacles, mussels and other sedentary organisms. The construction pattern and area is about 100 x 50 m. The actual area covered by the ruins may be much larger.

The Pallava dynasty (7th-9th centuries AD) of Tamil Nadu ruled the area during the period and constructed many rock-cut and constructed temples in Mahabalipuram and Kanchipuram. A tentative time frame for the ruins is the same as those of the temples in the vicinity. The problem from various angles such as a palaeo-shoreline and geology in addition to the archaeological aspects should be studied to shed more light on these discoveries. Further investigations will be carried out to determine the role of sea-level fluctuations, coastal erosion and neo-tectonic activities in affecting shoreline changes in the area during the recent past. The site has great potential for further exploration. A lot more remains to be done. If archaeological evidence proves these to be temple ruins and not natural phenomena, we still need to understand the cause of submergence of the structures and ensure that these are consistent with palaeo-oceanographic understanding of the area.

Onshore Exploration

Onshore exploration along the coast of Orissa, Andhra Pradesh, Tamil Nadu, Goa, Maharashtra, Gujarat and Lakshadweep has provided ample evidence on the maritime archaeology of India. The discoveries and observations of the exploration are briefly described.

Archaeological exploration and excavation provide detailed information about the cultural deposit of sites and their period. Keeping this in view, exploration was carried out along the Coast of Chilika Lake at Manikapatna, Palur, and the surrounding regions. Exploration was carried out at Manikapatna port to understand its location, environment and maritime contacts with other countries. Exploration brought to light black and red ware, red ware and glazed ware. Terracotta ring wells were seen at Manikapatna on the shore of Lake Chilika, which submerge during high tide and are exposed during low water. A diamond-shaped sandstone artefact (7 x 5 x 4 cm) having a plain base, with a little portion of its lower side broken and appearing like a mould, was found during explorations at Manikapatna. It has linear designs on it and resembles a stylised lotus flower motif datable to the 2nd to 8th centuries AD. It was possibly in a central position in a wall decoration or used for impressing decorations on pottery.

The exploration of ports and coastal trade centres of Andhra Pradesh, namely at Kalingapatnam, Salihundam and Dantapura yielded Rouletted ware, black and red ware and red ware. It appears that Dantapura is older than Kalingapatnam. Dantapura was deserted due to the change of course of the River Vamsadhara and Kalingapatnam came into importance. At Kalingapatnam local people informed us that there are some structures lying under water, which hinder navigation. However, they were unable to provide more details of these structures. Similar exploration was carried out at Buddhist sites, namely Bavikonda, Thotlakonda and Bimlipatnam. Earlier excavations at these trade centres had yielded stupas and monasteries. Rock-cut wells were noticed at Bavikonda and Thotlakonda. Thotlakonda is situated very close to the Bay of Bengal and might have served as a landmark in navigation. A lighthouse of AD 1864 was noticed at Bimlipatnam. A Dutch settlement had been established on the Buddhist ruins at Bimlipatnam. A wall constructed during the Dutch period is lying in the intertidal region, which indicates the region is prone to erosion.

Onshore exploration in and around Poompuhar region brought to light ring wells along with megalithic black and red ware. A few ring wells were also noticed near Vanagiri, Poompuhar and Tranquebar. A Sangam period (3rd century BC to 3rd century AD) brick structure was exposed near the present Kannagi statue. Another brick structure was noticed in the intertidal zone during low tide. These suggest that the shoreline is moving landward and a large part of the ancient city of Poompuhar must have been submerged in the sea.

A mid-17th century Danish map of Tranquebar, south of Poompuhar, shows a complete plan of the town along with the then shoreline. A careful study of the map suggests that Tranquebar town was well protected by a seaward fort wall and the Siva temple was sufficiently landward within the fort wall. It is estimated that during the 17th century AD the shoreline was at least 50 m away from the fort wall and a temple was located around 250-300 m from the shoreline. This observation unequivocally suggests that the shoreline has transgressed about 300 m in the last 300 years encroaching at an average rate of one metre per year. If the same trend has continued for the last 2,000 years, it might be expected that the ancient city of Poompuhar would have been submerged in 5 to 10 m of water off present day Poompuhar.

During maritime archaeological exploration five single hole stone anchors made of sandstone were found in the near shore and offshore off Manapad, Tamil Nadu. These anchors were used for *Toni* and *Vallam*. A stone quarry for making anchors was also noted close to the church of Manapad. This is the first evidence of a stone quarry for making anchors in India. Local people (not fishermen) were manufacturing these types of anchors which were rectangular in shape with a single hole. These anchors are still used as moorings for small fishing boats.

An Indo-Arabian type of stone anchor was noticed at Kannur, Kerala near the Hydross Palli Mosque during exploration. Half of the anchor is buried in the ground, but two square holes are visible. A thick coat of grey paint has been applied to its surface. The anchor is made of granite and it has been trimmed neatly by chisel leaving prominent straight lines all around on its surface. A big piece has been chipped from one side of the base, but there are no signs of wear. It seems to have been embedded in the ground at the same time as the construction of the mosque.

Onshore exploration and trial dig at Gopakapattana yielded laterite walls which are running perpendicular and parallel to the river Zuari. In one of the walls there are several bastions at regular intervals. Six stone steps attached to the main walls lead towards the shore. Explorations at Gopakapattana so far have not revealed any datable findings that could help determine how old these structures are. However, artefacts such as Roman coins and Chinese ceramics found in Gopakapattana and its adjoining regions, which have been displayed at the Pilar Museum, show that Gopakapattana was an ancient port. Similarly, exploration along the bank of the River Mandovi at Old Goa has yielded a number of Chinese ceramics datable to the Portuguese period.

Onshore exploration of Vijaydurg brought to light a dockyard about 3 km from Vijaydurg on the riverbank of Vaghotan. The length and width of the dock is 108 x 69 m respectively. The entrance of the dock is 7 m wide and made of dry masonry. Important finds include a number of Indo-Arabian types of stone anchors around the dockyard. It appears that these anchors were used as mooring bitts when the dock was in use. Similarly, these types of stone anchors have been used as the lintel of the niches of the outer wall of Vijaydurg fort. Both ends of the anchors are embedded in the wall and only the central portions are visible. Alternative uses of stone anchors have been noticed for the first time along the Maharashtra coast. Further, one composite type of stone anchor has been reported from Vijaydurg.

Exploration brought to light composite and Indo-Arabian stone anchors at Sindhudurg Fort, Malwan. These stone anchors have been embedded in the platform of the jetty of the Sindhudurg Fort whereas two Indo-Arabian stone anchors were used as mooring bitts where canoes are now tied. Another Indo-Arabian stone anchor was noticed at the entrance used as a lintel of Padamgad Fort, which served as the shipyard of Shivaji, the Maratha king. All these anchors are made of locally available laterite and sandstone and are highly weathered. It appears that these anchors had been in use prior to the construction of the fort by Shivaji. During the 17th century iron anchors were used extensively and stone anchors were abandoned. The surfaces of these anchors have undergone substantial weathering following exposure to the weather and are being used as paving stone. The discovery of stone anchors from Vijaydurg and Sindhudurg suggests that these were important maritime centres of India in the past.

Explorations at the habitation site of Sopara brought to light Black and Red ware, Red Polished ware (RPW) and Islamic glazed ware. Ancient remains were noticed in the area between the stupa and creek of Sopara. The exploration at Morabandar off Elephanta Island yielded 24 lead coins and Red ware sherds. The largest number of coins belongs to the Kalachuri dynasty (AD 550-575). Sherds of RPW, brick structures and large-size bricks were noted at Shetbandar off Elephanta Island. During onshore exploration four Indo-Arabian types of stone anchors were seen near the port office of Dhabol. These had been recovered during dredging near the jetty for the movement of passenger ships. The anchors are of different sizes, made of different rocks; marine growth is present on all of them. In one of the anchors two wooden flukes were present and the C14 dating of the timber suggests that the timber is 590±90 and 600±70 years old. On the basis of comparative study the Indo-Arabian stone anchors of India has been dated to the medieval period, between 8th and 16th centuries AD and beyond.

Onshore exploration in and around the Porbandar region of Gujarat brought to light for the first time the remains of a late Harappan settlement dating back to the 16th-14th centuries BC. This provides additional evidence to suggest that the Harappan legacy of maritime activity continued until the late Harappan period along the Saurashtra coast. The discovery of jetties along Porbandar creek signifies the importance of Porbandar as an active centre of maritime activities in the past. Probably these jetties were built during the medieval period. The siltation of the creek and the emergence of a new port in Porbandar are the important causes of disuse of these jetties. The present exploration has opened up a new horizon for further offshore exploration in Porbandar region.

Similarly, exploration at Mithi Virdi in Talaja taluka of Gujarat has yielded the biggest Indo-Arabian type of stone anchors ever reported from anywhere in the world. The stone anchors are unique in many ways and open up a new dimension in the study of stone anchors. They lack upper holes, which is puzzling to understand their proper function. Onshore exploration at Pindara brought to light the remains of a temple complex which is lying in the intertidal zone. The archaeological evidence shows progression of the shoreline during the last 1,000 years in this region. However, it is hard to attribute the reasons for the submergence of the temple; minor changes in sea level or seismic activity might have played a crucial role in its submergence.

Onshore artefacts from Kavaratti, Androth and Kadmat Island of Lakshadweep suggest that these islands were inhabited long before the Early Historical Period. Earlier exploration revealed Buddha heads from Minicoy Island. Red Polished Ware (RPW), red ware, black ware, dull red ware and buff ware were recorded at Kavaratti, Androth and Agatti. Further, Red ware and coarse grey ware belonging to the Medieval and Early Historical Period were also found at Amini.

Conclusion

Submerged sites and sunken shipwrecks are our cultural heritage. It is critical for us to decipher the records and link the past with the present. The rampant development activities in the coastal and offshore zone may destroy the evidence of past civilization forever. It is therefore imperative to make maritime archaeological investigations mandatory in the coastal zone, where any kind of developmental activity is taking place, such as development of ports, harbours, industry and tourism. In India very few shipwrecks have been explored. However, the rate of salvage of shipwrecks is high. Unless this salvaging is stopped it will cause the permanent destruction of evidence. On the other hand, submerged port and shipwreck sites can be promoted for tourism. Whenever any kind of archaeological remains are found, they should be immediately reported to the archaeological authorities; because once the evidence is lost it can never be recovered.

India has a 7516.6 km long coastline (including Andaman and Nicobar and Lakshadweep Islands) but only a fraction of its area has been explored. Onshore exploration has been carried out at different sites whereas underwater exploration has been confined to limited sites. Unless underwater exploration is carried out in the future the submerged and buried remains cannot be brought to light and those may reveal some clues of the maritime glory of our country.

SELECTED BIBLIOGRAPHY

Dhavalikar, M. K., 1977-78. An early warehouse on the western coast. *Puratattva*, Vol. 9: 100-103.

Gaur, A. S., Sila Tripati., 2006. Marine archaeological explorations on the southwestern coast of Saurashtra, India. *Journal of Indian Ocean Archaeology*, Vol. 3: 81-89.

Gaur, A. S., Sundaresh., and Sila Tripati., 2005. Marine archaeological investigations along the Saurashtra coast, west coast of India. *Journal of the Asiatic Society of Bangladesh*, Vol. 50: 159-195.

Gaur, A. S., Sundaresh., and Sila Tripati., 2004. An ancient harbour at Dwarka: Study based on the recent underwater explorations. *Current Science*, Vol. 86 (9): 1256- 1260.

Gaur, A. S., Sundaresh., and Sila Tripati., 2004. Stone anchors (composite type) from the Saurashtra coast, India: an indicator of ancient ports and sea routes. *Bulletin of the Australasian Institute for Maritime Archaeology*, Vol. 28: 125-132.

Gaur, A. S., Sundaresh; Sila Tripati., Bandodkar, S. N., 2002. Ring stone anchors from Gujarat, west coast of India. *Mariner's Mirror*, Vol. 88(4): 390-404.

Gaur, A. S., Sundaresh, Gudigar, P., Sila Tripati., Vora, K. H., and Bandodker, S. N., 2000. Recent Underwater explorations at Dwarka and surroundings of Okha Mandal. *Man and Environment*, Vol. XXV (1): 67-74.

Rao, S. R., 2001. *Marine Archaeology in India*. Publications Division, New Delhi.

Rao, S.R., 1999. *The Lost City of Dvaraka*. Aditya Prakashan, New Delhi.

Rao, S.R., 1990. Excavation of the legendary city of Dvaraka in the Arabian Sea. *Journal of Marine Archaeology*, Vol. 1: 59-98.

Rao, S. R., Sila Tripati., and Gaur, A. S., 1992. A Preliminary Exploration of Prabhasa - Somnath. *Journal of Marine Archaeology*, Vol. 3: 13-16.

Sila Tripati., Gaur, A. S., and Sundaresh., 2006. Exploration of a Portuguese shipwreck in Goa waters, western coast of India. *Bulletin of the Australasian Institute for Maritime Archaeology*, Vol. 30: 127-136.

Sila Tripati., Vora, K. H., 2005. Maritime heritage in and around Chilika Lake, Orissa: Geological evidences for its decline. *Current Science*, Vol. 88 (7): 1175-1181.

Sila Tripati., Manikfan, A., and Mohamed, M., 2005. An Indo-Arabian type of stone anchor from Kannur, Kerala, west coast of India. *International Journal of Nautical Archaeology*, Vol. 34 (1): 131-137.

Sila Tripati., Gaur, A. S., and Sundaresh., 2004, Marine Archaeology in India. *Man and Environment*, Vol. 29 (1): 28-41.

Sila Tripati., Parthiban, G., Vora, K. H., Sundaresh., and Bandodker, S. N., 2003. Lead ingots from a shipwreck off Poompuhar, Tamil Nadu, East Coast of India: evidence for overseas trade and their significance. *International Journal of Nautical Archaeology*, Vol. 32 (2): 225-237.

Sila Tripati., Gaur, A. S., and Sundaresh., 2003. Anchors from Goa waters, Central West Coast of India: Remains of Goa's overseas trade contacts with Arabian countries and Portugal. *Bulletin of the Australasian Institute for Maritime Archaeology*, Vol. 27: 97-106.

Sila Tripati., Sundaresh., Gaur, A. S., Gudigar, P., Bandodker, S. N., 2003. Exploration of Basel Mission Company shipwreck remains at St George's Reef off Goa, West Coast of India: impact of the Basel Mission Co. on society and culture. *International Journal of Nautical Archaeology*, Vol. 32 (1): 111-120.

Sila Tripati., 2002. Early maritime activities of Orissa on the east coast of India: Linkages in trade and cultural developments. *Man and Environment*, Vol. 27 (1): 117-126.

Sila Tripati., Sundaresh., Vora, K. H., and Bandodker, S. N., 2002. Marine Archaeological Research in India. *Indian Archaeology in Retrospect, Archaeology and Historiography*, Vol. IV, (Eds.), S. Settar and Ravi Korisettar, ICHR & Manohar, New Delhi: 353-392.

Sila Tripati., and Gudigar, P., 2001. Shipwreck archaeology of the Lakshadweep Islands, west coast of India. *International Journal of Nautical Archaeology*, Vol. 30 (1): 37-47.

Sila Tripati., 1999. Marine investigations in the Lakshadweep Islands, India. *Antiquity*, Vol. 73 (282): 827-835.

Sila Tripati., Saxena, M. K., Sundaresh., Gudigar, P., and Bandodkar, S. N., 1998. Marine archaeological exploration and excavation of Vijaydurg - a naval base of the Maratha Period, Maharashtra, on the west coast of India. *International Journal of Nautical Archaeology*, Vol. 27 (1): 51-63.

Sila Tripati., Gaur, A. S., Sundaresh, and Gudigar, P., 1996. Marine archaeological explorations in the Kaveripoompattinam region: Fresh light on the structural remains. *Man and Environment*, Vol. XXI (1): 86-90.

Sundaresh., Gaur, A. S., Sila Tripati., and Vora, K. H., 2004. Underwater investigations off Mahabalipuram, Tamil Nadu, India. *Current Science*, Vol. 86 (9): 1231- 1237.

Sundaresh., Gaur, A. S., Sila Tripati., Gudigar, P., and Bandodker, S. N., 2002. Stone anchors from Bet Dwarka Island, Gujarat coast, India: Significance to historical period maritime activities. *Bulletin of the Australasian Institute for Maritime Archaeology*, Vol. 26: 43-50.

Vora, K. H., 1987. A note on geophysical explorations for marine archaeology off Tamil Nadu coast, India. *International Journal of Nautical Archaeology*, Vol. 16 (2): 159-64.

1992. *Planets, Earth and Universe.* Duncan Brewer Publisher, Marshall Cavendish Corporation, Avon, UK.

1991. *Reader's Digest, Did you know*. London.

SOME FACTS OF MARITIME ARCHAEOLOGY AND RELATED ASPECTS OF THE SEA

1. India is one of the earliest maritime nations of the world. Harappans had trade relations with Persian Gulf countries and sailed along the coast of the Arabian Sea. The representation of boats on seals and potsherds confirms that there was strong seafaring activity during Harappan times and those boats were flat bottomed and had a sharp upturned prow and stern.
2. The Harappans were the earliest mariners of India. Harappan type seals, stone weights and semiprecious stone beads have been found variously in Bahrain, Failaka and Oman in the Arabian Peninsula and Ur, Kish and Brak in Iraq and Hissar and Susa in Iran. The occurrence of Harappan chessmen in the tomb of Queen Hatshepsut and Egyptian terracotta models of mummy and gorilla in the excavations at Lothal are evidence of overseas contacts during the 3rd millennium BC.
3. Harappan period shipwreck has been excavated at Ras Al Junayz, 200 km southeast of Muscat. Along with shipwreck, pottery, lumps of bitumen, most of them with imprints of reed bundles, ropes, mats and other objects have been excavated. The ship could be 20 m long and may have been built and sailed by the seafarers of the Harappan period.
4. Egyptians, Harappans, Greeks, Romans were skilled boat builders. They set sail around the Mediterranean, Indian Ocean, Persian Gulf and Red Sea to develop new trade links, to conquer new territories, to spread their religion and other aspects of human culture.

5. The dockyard of Lothal is the earliest tidal dock of India. It is a trapezoidal basin measuring 214 m x 36 m and enclosed by walls of kiln-fired bricks with sluice gates that enabled ships to enter at high tide through the inlet channel that was 12 m wide.
6. On the basis of seals and terracotta amulet of Harappa and Mohenjodaro it is believed that square type sails were used by the Harappans. Probably, the earliest date of square sail is 3100 BC which is depicted on the vase of Naqada, Egypt. However, Roman art strongly suggests that Mediterranean sails were square or rectangular. This could also be true in the case of the Red Sea.
7. In India, maritime archaeology started at the National Institute of Oceanography (NIO), Goa, a constituent laboratory of CSIR, in 1981 with the object of excavating the rich underwater heritage lying close to our shores.
8. The Mediterranean Sea is the birthplace of maritime archaeology. It was in the Mediterranean Sea that a lot of artefacts were found by fishermen and later excavated by archaeologists. Underwater explorations are still being carried out in the Mediterranean Sea.
9. In India the first maritime archaeological exploration started off Dwarka, Gujarat, West coast of India in 1982-83, which brought to light the remains of an ancient port. Dwarka was a busy trading port till the medieval period.
10. Underwater explorations and excavations off Dwarka have yielded the largest number (one hundred twenty three) of stone anchors in the world. They comprised of composite (triangular), Indo-Arabian, Ring stone and single hole type and were made of miliolite limestone, sandstone, basalt, dolerite, etc
11. Poompuhar, the Sangam Period (3rd century BC to 3rd century AD) Chola port town, is the first site on the east coast of India where maritime archaeological explorations have been carried out and underwater remains have been recorded.
12. The exploration at Mithi Virdi in Talaja taluka of Gujarat has yielded five very large (4.9 m length and average estimated weight 3800 kg) Indo-Arabian stone anchors ever reported in the world. These anchors were found in agricultural land one km away from the present shoreline.

13. In Indian waters so far no lead stock anchors have been found. However, lead stock anchors were used extensively by the Romans and Greeks since 5th and 4th centuries BC. Many lead stocks have been found in the Mediterranean Sea and North Atlantic Sea.
14. The first underwater evidence of Roman contacts with India comes from the finds off Bet Dwarka, Gujarat coast which includes amphorae (handles and bases), ring stone type lead anchors and a bun shaped lead ingot.
15. The excavations of Berenike and Myos Hormos ports on the Red Sea coast of the early historical period have yielded the fragment remains of sails made of Indian cotton. Large pieces of sail were also recovered in the burial grounds at Thebes, Berenike and their reconstruction roughly suggests that they could be rectangular. In addition to this, Indian pottery, coins, Tamil-Brahmi and Sanskrit-Prakrit inscriptions, black pepper and coconuts have also been recovered from these sites.
16. Various types of boats are depicted on the seals, coins, caves, stupas and temple walls of India but it is difficult to know their exact sizes because these depictions provide only the plan but not the elevation of the ship. In the absence of their length, height and width it is difficult to estimate the exact size and differentiate between river going and seagoing vessels.
17. Through the centuries various types of pots (amphorae, earthen jars, celadon jars, Chinese ceramic jars and Martaban jars) were used for transporting both liquid and solid materials on boats and ships. But in the Indian context the earliest evidence of carrying of pottery onboard comes from the Ajanta paintings (6th century AD).
18. The bas relief found in the tomb of king Sahu-re at Abusir, dateable 3000 BC, depicts a boat on which stone anchors are shown on the prow. Similarly, a ship has been depicted on a Cypriot jug (7th century BC) showing a crewman lowering the ring stone type of anchor from the bow.
19. Like the depiction of boats on the potsherds, terracotta seals, paintings and cave walls of India, there are also ship graffiti on the potsherds of Berenike on Red Sea coast and Tissamaharama of Sri Lanka, a sailing craft in an early Brahmi inscription from Duvegala, Sri Lanka, on terracotta seal and stucco of Nakhon Pathom, Thailand and in the cave wall of Socotra. The boat of Socotra resembles the painting of cave No. 2 of Ajanta.

20. Like stone anchors and two handled jugs 'amphoras' are important aspects of maritime archaeology. Amphoras still exist especially in the rural areas of Anatolia, Turkey. The people of these regions have not abandoned the individual shapes of amphoras and those are the representatives of 5000 years old maritime heritage.
21. In Egypt shallow bottomed boats made of reeds with a single sail, carried cargo and passengers along the River Nile. After about 2700 BC the Egyptians began to build wooden boats which were stronger and could cross the open seas to reach foreign lands.
22. Phoenician ships were short, broad and strong. They were built from Cedar, which grew on the mountain slopes of Phoenicia. A single sail and oars powered the ship. Around 1400 BC Phoenicians became excellent seafarers sailing great distances in search of trade and commerce.
23. Initially Arabs avoided the Southern Indian Ocean calling it the 'Sea of Darkness'. The main type of ships used by the Arabs for their travels was the dhow. It had one or two masts and a triangular sail bent on to a spar. This was called a lateen sail. Dhow is a versatile ship which can carry a large volume of cargo.
24. Until the 15th century, most of the European ships were square-rigged which meant they could only sail in much the same direction as the wind. Most of the great explorers, including Columbus used small ships called 'caravel' which had triangular 'lateen' sails adopted from Arab dhows. With these sails, a caravel could sail almost directly into the wind.
25. Earlier explorers had used square sailed ships, which were limited in their manoeuvrability. The development of new technology such as the caravel type ship with triangular 'lateen' sails which could sail almost directly into the wind opened up new possibilities.
26. The exploration of a shipwreck in the early 1960s off the Great Basses Reef in Southeast coast of Sri Lanka near Kirinda by Arthur C. Clarke and Mike Wilson yielded sacks of silver coins of Aurangzeb (1658-1707) minted in Surat, Gujarat in 1701. British bronze cannon and flintlock pistols were also found along with these coins.
27. The Sunchi Reef shipwreck off Goa coast is the first and the oldest (early 17th century) so far explored in Indian waters. The shipwreck findings confirm the evidence regarding Indo-Portuguese maritime trade and commerce.

28. The earliest shipwreck so far explored is the '*Uluburun*', off Turkey, datable to the 14th century BC in 60 m water depth by INA and Texas A&M University, USA. Excavations continued for 11 summer seasons from 1984 and 22400 dives were made.
29. The deepest shipwreck so far explored is the '*Titanic*' located in 1985 in 3798 m (12460 ft) water depth. Seven expeditions were carried out over nine years jointly by the Wood Hole Oceanographic Institution, Massachusetts and the *Institut Francais de recherch pour I'exploitation de la mer* (IFREMER), France led by Robert Ballard and Jean Louis Michael.
30. *Titanic* sank in the North Atlantic hit by an iceberg on 14 April 1912. Its length was 269 m, displacement 66000 tons, speed 24-25 knots. It was carrying a total of 2207 passengers including crew and 705 survived.
31. Accounts of foreign travellers and marine records state that Indian spices such as pepper, clove and cinnamon were in great demand in Europe since ancient times. The *Nossa Senhora dos Martires* (1606) ship was carrying pepper which was brought to light during the recent excavations in the River Tejos, off Lisbon. These peppers were lying on the riverbed.
32. Europeans introduced iron anchors in India. It is only from the Seventeenth century onwards that the uses of iron anchors were evident in Indian waters. Since then both stone and iron anchors were used simultaneously.
33. Indian teak was largely used in shipbuilding and was sought after by the people of Middle East and later by the Europeans. In a later period Europeans replaced oak and pine with Indian teak in shipbuilding industry because of its versatility and high quality.
34. On arrival in India the Portuguese found that the locals were using coir ropes for anchor handling. Coir rope was more functional as it absorbed less water than hemp rope used by the Portuguese mariners. Subsequently Portuguese encouraged the use coir rope in shipping and shipbuilding.
35. The bell of an Indian built ship that was recovered from Ruapuke beach, New Zealand, appears to be 500 years old. The bell has a Tamil inscription which reads, 'the bell of Moha Din Buksh's ship'. Presently, the bell is in Dominion Museum, Wellington. This shows that during 14th and 15th centuries Indians already had trade contacts with the Pacific Ocean islands.

36. Academically, maritime archaeology started around 1960. Archaeologists like Peter Throckmorton, George Bass, Joan du Plat Taylor, Honor Frost and others were responsible for promoting interest in this new field.
37. Professor George F. Bass (born 1932) in Columbia, South Carolina, USA is the founding father of Maritime Archaeology. He founded the Institute of Nautical Archaeology (INA) in 1973. INA is a non-profit organisation and involved in exploration of several shipwrecks and submerged habitational sites around the world.
38. Peter Throckmorton (1928 - 1990) was the first scholar to take archaeology to the seabed. Throckmorton was a founding member of the Sea Research Society. He has discovered several shipwrecks in the Mediterranean Sea.
39. Commandant Jacques Yves Cousteau (1910-1997) with his invention of the aqualung revolutionised underwater diving. He was a multifaceted man, as an author he has written more than 50 books and as a researcher he has studied the sea and all forms of life in water.
40. S. R. Rao (born 1922) in Shimoga district of Karnataka is known as the father of Maritime archaeology of India. He has worked on various aspects of Indian Archaeology. He started Maritime Archaeology after his retirement from Archaeological Survey of India.
41. Slyvia Earle has spent more than 6000 hrs underwater and has photographed or documented more than 20000 marine species. She holds a record for the deepest (318 m) unconnected human dive in history.
42. Keith Muckelroy (1951-1980), a leading UK maritime archaeologist, ironically drowned in shallow water on 8th September 1980 in a diving accident in Loch Tay, Scotland. His contributions to maritime archaeology are significant.
43. To date not a single maritime archaeologist has been attacked by a shark. It is interesting to note that out of 350 species of shark only 27 species have been accused in attacks on humans. Most sharks are non-offensive animals and do not threaten divers.
44. The simplest tool used for protection from shark is 'shark billy'; it is a 1.5 m long stick with a steel tip that can be used to poke at the sensitive snouts of oncoming sharks. Should a shark pick you as a prey, his teeth could snap that billy like a dry twig, but since his first approach is usually a scouting

expedition, the poke on the snout is ordinarily enough to discourage him. Even electrical shark deterrent devices are available which are used to discourage sharks from approaching divers.

45. While diving, it is always better to avoid going near sea animals (shark, barracuda, stingrays, jellyfish, lionfish, stonefish, scorpion fish, sea snakes, stinging hydroid, sea urchins and corals) which may cause harm.

46. It has been experienced whilst diving in Dwarka waters that when a grouper fish is driven out from the working site, it later comes back with a school of groupers, they encircle the divers and keep a watch on what the divers do, this could indicate that either they are afraid of divers or do not like intruders in their area.

47. Maritime archaeology has an exceptional safety record. The early diving expeditions off the coast of Turkey, where G. F. Bass and others have dived with air support to considerable depths, where only one or two minor cases of the bends have been reported. There are a few cases of diving accidents in which archaeologists and volunteers have died off Sicily in Italy, Giglio shipwreck, Italy and Mary Rose project, UK.

48. Maritime Archaeology is a multidisciplinary science. For instance, the discovery of a shipwreck is studied, assembled, preserved and exhibited in a museum. In order to understand the problems, collaboration of chemists, physicians, oceanographers, ocean engineers, nautical architects, photographers, designers and laboratory technicians are required. Many of them participate for contributing to the process of restoring and learning from these finds which come from the sea.

49. In terms of Oceanography, the Black Sea is thought to have received its name because of the layer of hydrogen sulphide beginning about 200 meters below the surface and supporting a unique microbial population which produces black sediments probably due to anaerobic methane oxidation. Strabo (60 BC-19 AD) believed that the Black Sea was called 'inhospitable' because it was difficult to navigate and inhabited by savage tribes on its shores.

50. The Dead Sea is land locked between Israel and Jordan, on the river Jordan. It is the world's lowest body of water on earth (420 m below MSL). It is called 'dead' because of its high salinity which prevents macroscopic aquatic organisms, such as fishes and aquatic plants, from living in it, though tiny

quantities of bacteria and microbial fungi are found. The salinity is eight times saltier than other sea waters and high density makes for a harsh environment where living organisms cannot flourish.

51. Among the sciences, physics is most relevant to diving since it deals with density and buoyancy factor of the water. However, some principles of physics such as gravity is passive and others regarding vision and hearing may be misleading, as colour perception changes with change of depth pertaining to the diving environment and their influence on the diver. The refractive effect of light causes objects to appear larger and closer under water. However, overestimation occurs at distances greater than a meter.
52. 10 m water depth is equivalent to 1 unit pressure: it is relevant when a diver ascends too rapidly from a high pressure area to low pressure area. As it can result in pressure related problems e.g., bends, damage to eardrums, etc.
53. In diving, both inhaling and exhaling are done through the mouth, because the nose is covered with a mask. Whenever divers feel a dry sensation in the throat, they take out the mouth piece and intake a little water and put the mouth piece back again.
54. Lead is preferred and used for weight belts by divers because of its specific gravity and its weight. It is worn on the belt to offset positive buoyancy and achieve neutral buoyancy. It is advisable to use approximate weight belts to avoid discomfort underwater.
55. It is never advisable to dive alone, always dive with a buddy and plan your dives with your buddy before diving. During diving one buddy should be responsible for keeping track of the other and they should never be separated under water.
56. In shallow water diving, compressed air (oil and moisture-free) is used while a mixture of helium and oxygen is used for deep water diving. In deep water diving, the diver should take care of the duration of dive and water depth.
57. Nitrogen Narcosis: when a diver descends using compressed air, at about 30 to 40 m, he or she starts experiencing nitrogen narcosis; this is because of the absorption of nitrogen narcosis into the cells of the central nervous system. When narcosis occurs divers tend to get hallucinated.

58. In the surf zone (the area between wave breaker zone to the shore is known as surf zone), it is often wiser and easier to swim all the way to the shore and crawl out of water than to stand and try to walk.
59. The pressure changes associated with space travel is much less than those associated with travel into the depths of the ocean. Never fly soon after diving, for it may cause pressure problems; one should wait for at least 12 hours before flying.
60. Never take alcoholic beverages and drugs when you are diving because they can affect your ability to dive. Diving under these influences is extremely hazardous.
61. Avoid diving if you are suffering from a cold or fever and never insist on some one diving if he or she is not willing to do so. One should be in good health in order to dive.
62. In diving women have some special health considerations. Women are more susceptible to decompression sickness than men, they should be more conservative with time and depth limits.
63. Ordinary pencil, acrylic boards or polyester tracing (Garware) film and measuring tape are used for preparation of sketches, underwater drawings and documentations.
64. The basic differences between land and underwater cameras are that 'O' rings are provided at every joint in underwater cameras which prevent water seepage into the lenses. Otherwise, mechanically both are the same.
65. Video cameras are also used for underwater videography in a housing which is a watertight chamber. Unlike still cameras, video cameras must always be held horizontally.
66. Sound travels faster underwater and is non-directional. It is difficult to determine the direction of the sound. However, sound is only used to call the divers up.
67. In many countries youngsters know about diving and participate in shipwreck diving organised by universities, institutes and professional societies. Some dive for pleasure for viewing flora and fauna but this is not so in India because of the lack of awareness and facilities.

68. Excavating under water has disadvantages but also advantages - the excavator can hover over his/her trench and spoil is much easier to remove.

69. Much more time is spent above water, drawing and photographing finds, making records, etc., than is spent working under water for the same. Diving itself is not stressful or energetic, though getting in and out of the water and handling the equipment can be!

70. If any object or artefact is buried in the subsoil, it does not deteriorate fast, (Ref Table. 1) unlike artefact buried on the land or on the surface of the seabed. Nothing happens to some metals such as gold whether it is buried or lying on the seabed.

71. Before the introduction of electronic devices for underwater communications, divers used hand signals to communicate. These signals are still prevalent. Each signal has its own meaning and is universal.

72. If we look into the early modes of transportation man has been using various types of animals and birds (camel, donkey, elephant, horse, Llama, pigeon, yak, etc.) for the purpose but after gaining knowledge of water transport he felt it was easier, cheaper, faster and could carry more than land transport.

73. After venturing into the sea, men used rafts and canoes, then developed paddles and oars to propel the craft faster even against the wind and currents. The next step of invention was the masts and sails to propel the craft with wind and reduced use of muscle power.

74. The word navigate has been derived from the Latin word '*navis*' meaning 'ship' and '*agere*' meaning 'to move' or 'to direct'. In ancient times mariners found the direction by looking at the Sun and stars. To go towards east they looked towards the direction of the sun rise. Seamen have been using the positions of the constellations for navigation. The Pole Star which indicates North was especially useful to them.

75. For centuries together ships had to rely on strong oarsmen or on the wind and sail during their voyages. For instance, in calm weather, a ship could be becalmed for days together. Wooden hulled ships (sewn and nailed) were easily damaged after striking reefs and sand bars. Then, in the 1800s, the first steamship and steel hulled vessels were introduced and sea transport became much more reliable, easier and faster.

76. The first explorers had little to help them navigate apart from the positions of the Sun, Moon and stars and had to stay close to land. The development of instruments like the magnetic compass, astrolabe and quadrant made navigation easier and more exact.

77. The sextant gets its name from its shape, which is one sixth of a circle. The mirror sextant was developed in the mid 1700s to measure latitude accurately. It has one mirror that you point at the horizon and another mirror you adjust until the Sun or a star is reflected in it at exactly the same height as the horizon. The degree of adjustment you need to make to the second mirror gives the latitude. Sextant became the main navigational aid for sailors.

78. Pirates have been around the seas and oceans since ancient times as long as people have used them as trade routes. References to piracy come from the Assyrians, Egyptians and Phoenicians since 1900 BC, even Herodotus (490-429 BC), Ptolemy and ancient Indian texts mention Piracy.

79. Scholars believe that manmade factors such as weak successors, poor economic conditions, attack by neighbouring kingdoms, etc. were the causes of decline of ports and trade centres of India. Coastal erosion, tectonic activities, sedimentation and formation of sand bars in the navigational channels, etc. were also equally important factors for their decline. These are the real threats to existing coastal monuments along the coast of India.

80. There is enough water in the atmosphere to cover the entire surface of the earth with 25 mm (1") of water. The average temperature of the atmosphere at the surface of Earth is 150 C.

81. The tropics are the main engines of the Earth's rain system. Every year about 450,000 cubic kilometres (368000 cu miles) of water rise as vapour from the oceans heated by the sun. The vapour from clouds is eventually condensed by cooling which falls back to Earth as rain or snow.

82. Oxygen builds a protective barrier of ozone and this is a special form of oxygen that is found only in the upper level of the atmosphere which shields living things from the sun's ultraviolet rays.

83. 99 % of Antarctica's land mass is covered in ice which represents 9/10th of all the ice on earth. It is the fifth largest continent and about 1.3 times larger than Europe. The coastline of Antarctica measures 17,968 km mostly covered by ice formations.

84. Only 2.8% of the earth's water is fresh and of that a small portion (only 6%) is liquid and well over 90% is locked up in the polar ice caps and the remainder is water vapour in the atmosphere. About 98% of the earth's liquid fresh water is underground.

85. There is no living thing that does not contain some water. Plants need water to carry out photosynthesis and animals need water for digesting food, excreting waste and in the more complex species circulating blood. A lettuce leaf is 94% water, a human being 60 to 70% and a pine tree 55%.

86. The average depth of the ocean is 3800 m and the greatest depth is 11040 m. These depths are farther below sea level than the average and greatest elevations of the land are above sea level.

87. Water effectively absorbs all electromagnetic radiation including radio, radar, and visible light waves. Hence, oceanographers can 'see' through the ocean waters only by using sound waves which travel through water with relatively little absorption.

88. The oceans depths are a three-dimensional domain that remain for most part, unvisited and unexplored. The deepest point in the oceans is 11022 m (36160 ft) below sea level. It lies in the Marianas trench on the south west of Guam in the Pacific Ocean.

89. Earth is the only planet known to have water in all three states: solid (ice), liquid and gas (atmospheric vapour). The oceans contain 97% of the earth's water. They are in contact with and can exchange heat and water vapour with the atmosphere over more than 70% of the earth's surface. The transfer of heat and water vapour between the oceans and the atmosphere are the main driving forces that determine the world's climate.

90. Almost 25% of the solar radiation reaching the earth is absorbed and converted to heat in the atmosphere. About 50% is absorbed by the ocean and land and the rest is reflected back to space.

91. As with swimming, the diving abilities of animals put humans to shame. The deepest possible human breath-held dive without artificial aids is about 100 m (330 ft). Whereas the emperor penguins can reach depths of more than 260 m (850 ft) and remain underwater for 18 minutes.

92. Like whales and dolphins, humans can take a breath and descend into the deep waters of the seas. Majority of people can hold their breath for forty seconds; Tanya Streeter of USA can hold her breath for over six minutes. In the recent past she dived to the depth of 160 m in two and a half minutes.
93. The sperm whale has been recorded to a dive of 2250 m (7380 ft), a depth equivalent to 5 times the height of the Empire State Building. By contrast humans have only reached a depth of 686 m (2263 ft) using air tanks and pressurised suits.
94. The fastest fish in the ocean is the sailfish. By streamlining its body, it is capable of swimming at a speed of 100 km/h (60 mph), by comparison the fastest human swimmer can manage only about 8 km/h (5mph).
95. The salinity of water of the seas and oceans vary from region to region. But there is enough salt in the oceans to cover all the continents with a layer, 150 m (490 ft) thick.
96. In 325 BC the Greek Pytheas developed a means of determining latitude from the angular distance of the North Star and proposed a connection between the phases of the moon and the tides.
97. Ferdinand Magellan (1480-1521), the first circum navigator sailed from Spain to reach Spice Island (Moluccas) in the '*Victoria*' but he reached Philippine Islands by crossing the South Atlantic Ocean, around Cape Horn, across the Pacific. Similarly, Francis Drake (1543-1596), an English seafarer, the second person to sail round the world in the '*Pelican*' collected about 6 tonnes of clove from the Spice Islands.
98. In a true sense, the American engineer Robert Fulton made the first steam engine boat in 1807. The boat carried people and voyaged 240 km up the River Hudson between New York and Albany. In sailing ships this distance was covered in four days whereas Fulton's steamboat took less than a day.
99. In 1452-1519, Leonardo da Vinci observed, recorded and interpreted the characteristics of currents and waves and noted that fossils in the Italian mountains implied that sea level had been higher in the ancient past.

100. In 1569, Geradus Mercator constructed a map projection of the world that was adapted for navigational charts. In 1925-1927, A German expedition aboard the research vessel '*Meteor*' studied the physical oceanography of the Atlantic Ocean using an echo sounder extensively for the first time. In 1978, 'Seasat-A', the first oceanographic satellite was launched demonstrating the utility of remote sensing in the study of the oceans.